ABRAHAM OUR FATHER

ABRAHAM OUR FATHER

PAUL AND THE ANCESTORS IN POSTCOLONIAL AFRICA

ISRAEL KAMUDZANDU

Fortress Press
Minneapolis

ABRAHAM OUR FATHER

Paul and the Ancestors in Postcolonial Africa

Cover image: Marianos and Hanina (6th century CE). The Sacrifice of Isaac. Detail: Abraham. From the pavement of the Beth Alpha synagogue © Erich Lessing / Art Resource, NY

Cover design: Tory Herman

Library of Congress Cataloging-in-Publication Data

Print ISBN: 978-0-8006-9817-1

eBook ISBN: 978-1-4514-2629-8

The paper used in this publication meets the minimum requirements of American National Standard for Information Sciences — Permanence of Paper for Printed Library Materials, ANSI Z329.48-1984.

Manufactured in the U.S.A.

This book was produced using PressBooks.com, and PDF rendering was done by PrinceXML.

CONTENTS

Other Books in the Series

The Paul in Critical Contexts series offers cutting-edge reexaminations of Paul through the lenses of power, gender, and ideology.

Apostle to the Conquered
Reimagining Paul's Mission
Davina C. Lopez

The Arrogance of Nations
Reading Romans in the Shadow of Empire
Neil Elliott

Christ's Body in Corinth
The Politics of a Metaphor
Yung Suk Kim

Galatians Re-Imagined
Reading Paul through the Eyes of the Vanquished
Brigitte Kahl

The Politics of Heaven
Women, Gender, and Empire in the Study of Paul
Joseph A. Marchal

The Colonized Apostle
Paul through Postcolonial Eyes
Christopher D. Stanley, editor

Onesimus Our Brother
Reading Religion, Race, and Slavery in Philemon
Matthew V. Johnson, James A. Noel, and Demetrius K. Williams, editors

The Practice of Hope
Ideology and Intention in First Thessalonians
Néstor O. Míguez

Eros and the Christ
Longing and Envy in Paul's Christology
David E. Fredrickson

Acknowledgements

I would like to thank the following people who assisted and took part in the production process of this book.

First and foremost, I want to thank my colleague, mentor, and friend Professor Harold Washington, who encouraged me to continue doing research on postcolonial readings of the Bible, especially Pauline literature. His comments during our conversations greatly motivated me and set me on an adventure that resulted in this book.

Second, my former New Testament professors and colleagues who first read my dissertation and commented that I have at least five other books to be birthed from that dissertation: David Balch, Carolyn Osiek, Vincent Wimbush, Robert Jewett, Larry Wellborn, Thomas Dozeman, Dale Martin, Musa Dube, and Leo Perdue.

I especially thank Professor Balch, who constantly sends me new resources to read and use for this book, for his dedication to my growth in research and New Testament academic writing. He is indeed a great supporter, and I trust that my work holds up in his perspective. Larry Welborn, a former New Testament professor and now a colleague, has taught me much about Paul and continues to do so in generous ways. I have consulted with him many times over both phone and email. Although we have sometimes disagreed on postcolonial readings and interpretations of Paul, he has assisted me in strengthening and clarifying my arguments so as to be understood by a wider audience.

I would like to thank the Saint Paul School of Theology for granting me a sabbatical in the summer of 2011, which I used to do more research in Africa. It was a well-received sabbatical, and I will continually appreciate and treasure my work for this seminary, my colleagues, and my friends. I deeply thank the library staff at Saint Paul School of Theology for their careful assistance in getting interlibrary resources on time and for allowing me to extend the borrowing time. They are terrific people, and I look forward to their continued assistance.

Much appreciation is extended to acquisitions editor Neil Elliott, who met with me to discuss this project late one evening in a restaurant in New Orleans during an annual meeting of the Society of Biblical Literature. His comments and critique of the manuscript were in many ways challenging, but informative. Without his advice, support, and encouragement, this book would not have come to this final stage. I treasure his willingness to let me write as a postcolonial African Christian.

I thank my copyeditor and proofreader Mrs. Ruth Ann Wood for her diligence in reading and raising questions on each chapter. She is indeed an amazing theological copyeditor. I have benefited tremendously from her theological analysis, knowledge, and insight into Paul and the ancestry of Abraham.

Finally, I thank my wife, Rutendo Patricia, and my three daughters for their support when I was writing this book. I will be remiss if I do not mention my parents, who went to be with the Lord many years ago and now are my ancestors, whose voices continue to inspire me on this journey of life. May their souls rest in peace, and may their ancestral, prayerful voices be present in my life. This book is indeed a tribute to my family.

Preface

This book is about ancestry, spirituality, and culture among African Christians in colonial and postcolonial Zimbabwe—and about the surprising role the figure of the apostle Paul played in the colonial and postcolonial periods. The experiences of the colonized, the processes they reinvented or coped with, and how they identified themselves in relation to colonial forces are first on the agenda of postcolonial biblical interpretation. The claim is not that colonialism brought a new religion, but that the two, African traditional religion and colonialism, transformed each other. Beginning with the history of the identity of Shona people and their encounter with British colonialism and Euro-American missionaries, this study focuses on Shona Christianity as a deliberate, evolving, and constructed response born from an encounter with those forces. To say that Shona Christianity evolved invites a theological debate. I wish to center that debate on a comparison with the apostle Paul's creative construction of Abraham in the midst of the *Aeneadae*, by which I mean the Romans of the Augustan era whose identity was both politically and religiously grounded in the ancestry of Aeneas. Paul's Letter to the Romans is arguably the most influential Pauline epistle in the history of Christianity, yet its influence among cultures has not yet been fully explored. In this project, I will examine Paul's legacy within the context of colonial and postcolonial Zimbabwe.

The reading and interpretation of the Bible, especially Paul's Epistle to the Romans (3:27—4:25), awakened among the colonized Shona people a renewed sense of the role, function, and place of ancestors in religious worldviews. While precolonial Africans were aware of God prior to the introduction of Christianity, their reading and interpretation of Paul was formative and transformative in two ways. First, they discovered Paul to be a theological dialogue partner in matters of culture, ancestry, ethnicity, and spirituality. The gospel of Jesus Christ—which, Paul argues in Rom. 1:16 and 3:31, invites "all" into a right relationship with God through faith—was formative for the African religious worldview. As a religious people, African Christians saw their appropriation of "Father Abraham" not as a *universal* ancestor, but rather as the ancestor of a remnant. In this case, Abraham's entry into faith (Gen. 15:6) does not transcend and abolish differences, but rather confirms the diversity of Christian faith. Thus the concept of Abraham's people as a remnant drawn from Jews and non-Jews brings into sharp relief the evolution of Christianity among the Shona people. What is called out in Abraham is not universality, but a remnant. African Christianity is a new appropriation of Christian faith on the basis of the Messiah.

Next, the book will contextualize Paul within the worldview of African Christians. As a constructed response, Shona Christianity, which is multiethnic in nature, actively picked and chose what it received from missionaries. This intentional approach transformed colonial African Christianity to what Shona postcolonial critics now call postcolonial Christian faith. Thus encounter between colonialism and African religious systems cannot be separated from the arrival of the Bible. The Bible in Africa has always played a double-edged function: as a tool for colonizing and as an agent of transformation. The latter is what will be discovered as the book progresses. Paul, the apostle to the Gentiles, is indeed a major theological resource in the development of Christianity in postcolonial Zimbabwe.

Postcolonial analysis is interested in the relationship between the colonizers and the colonized. Thus, with regard to the first century, I will juxtapose Virgil's *Aeneid*, in which Augustus is presented as an advocate of cultural renewal through ancestral veneration, with Paul's presentation of Abraham as a competing ancestor of the Roman Empire. The story of Aeneas as told under the Julian-Claudian family resonates with the experiences of the African worldview. It is an experience of power, culture, and identity; realities that cultural practitioners will evolve into a new mode of religious existence. Seeing power through the prism of colonialism and missionary efforts provides a vivid means for looking at culture and cultural engagement with the gospel of Jesus Christ.

The study will in part engage the historical, literary, and ideological milieu of the Augustan era in the Roman Empire. The elements of prejudice and power toward inferior people seem to be a concern at the center of Paul's language in Romans. A postcolonial analysis of the legacy of Paul's Letter to the Romans in Zimbabwe is in order because it assists twenty-first-century Christian readers in southern Africa, especially Zimbabwe, who were once under the imperial claims of European colonialism, to appreciate the import of Romans as a missionary document. As a practitioner of postcolonial analysis, I will seek to address in this book the construction of the identity of the colonized and the processes of such constructions whose goal leads to the birth of a new phenomenon. The exposure of the colonized to the ideals of the colonizers leads to a shifting of identities. In this book, the new expression of Christianity that was born from the engagement of the colonizers with the colonized will be labeled postcolonial Christianity.

Beginning with chapter 1, the study will offer a historical account of the arrival of colonial and missionary groups in Zimbabwe. The perception of Africans on the part of both colonizers and missionaries was complex and dehumanizing. European colonialists and missionaries projected themselves as champions of Christian virtues and educators of human values. Their aim was to educate, evangelize, and produce an African who would be subordinate to the teachings of Western culture. In this case, this first chapter focuses on the arrival of British missionaries and their perception of African culture, which resulted in a period of encounter, engagement, confrontation, and transformation for all three parties: namely, the indigenous Shona people, colonial officials, and missionaries.

Chapter 2 will focus on religious cultural configurations and the intense engagement between African religion and missionary teachings. Colonial and missionary education, especially so-called moral and religious education, whether in public or missionary schools, was the incubator of African Christianity.

Chapter 3 will focus on identifying postcolonial Christianity in relation to its engagement with Paul as a theological figure in the colonial encounter. Paul's theological argument in Rom. 4:1-25 and the way Africans appropriated and engaged with his message of the gospel of Jesus Christ will be explored as a period not only of synthesis but also antisynthesis, leading to the birth of an authentic African Christianity. The new theology that Africans appropriated from Paul's gospel was a new understanding of Jesus, of which Paul is the first witness.

The fourth chapter will focus on the nature of postcolonial Christianity as a multiethnic African Christianity, both African and Christian, with a renewed understanding of the role, place, and function of ancestors. It will demonstrate the process and nature of African Shona Christianity's adaptation, faith, and spirituality. The chapter also describes the function of the cult of Aeneas in the Greco-Roman world and the ways in which Paul advanced his gospel using the language and culture of the day.

The fifth chapter presents the ways in which Hellenistic Judaism depicted the ancestral greatness of Abraham—ways similar to the Augustan use of the Aeneas legend. The Shona people, in their process of adaptation, already felt an affinity with Paul's idea of ancestry. Here the study will focus on Aeneas and Abraham. Shona people creatively appropriated selected aspects of Euro-American Christianity in their religion just as Paul had creatively interacted with his Greco-Roman context. Heretofore, Western New Testament scholarship has not seen this adequately because its practitioners have been at home in the dominant colonial culture. Indeed, the experience of colonization helped Shona Christians to recognize that Paul's appropriation of Abraham in the context of the Roman Empire was to counter the ideology of the Julian-Claudian family. A juxtaposition of Aeneas and Abraham will conclude the book with some theological and spiritual implications on the part of Shona postcolonial Christians of Zimbabwe.

Introduction

This book seeks to comprehend Paul's theology in the contexts of other cultures, more specifically a particular culture: postcolonial Christianity in Zimbabwe. This Christianity is not a stand-alone religion but a synthesis of Western and African cultures.[1] Missionaries and colonial forces in Zimbabwe during the colonial period (1890–1980) greatly overlooked the symbolic world of the Shona people and imposed a new culture on an already religious people. The Shona selectively and inventively appropriated parts of the colonial version of Christianity that missionaries offered them and then transformed it. One important element in that critical appropriation was the figure of Abraham. The way Shona Christians came to understand Abraham as an ancestor has important resonance with the way Paul originally sought to present Abraham in the context of an alternative ancestor myth.

I will argue that Paul's exegesis of the Genesis story in Romans 4 cannot be appreciated without taking into account the influence of the *Aeneid*—Virgil's Roman epic, meant to celebrate the religious and political foundations of Augustus (26 BCE–68 CE). I wish to use the interaction of Aeneas and Abraham traditions of Paul's time as an analogy for the growth of Christianity in precolonial, colonial, and postcolonial Africa.

Aeneas and Abraham were founding ancestors of their respective peoples, and yet no significant effort has been made to study Paul's engagement with the Roman Empire through his appropriation of Abraham as a spiritual ancestor of "all" faith people in Romans. In this case, Virgil's *Aeneid* and Paul's Epistle to the Romans have a dialogical theological relationship that illuminates the apostle's message among "Gentiles."[2] Paul not only builds on an apologetic tradition in Hellenistic Judaism but also interacts with an ideological trend in early Roman imperialism, which found in the tradition of Aeneas a basis for reconciling Greeks and Romans. Therefore, Paul's portrayal of Abraham as an ancestor of Jews and Greeks alike is an ideological construct analogous to the propaganda of the Augustan age (26 BCE–68 CE), with which his Roman audience would have been familiar. Yet, by asserting that Abraham the Jew, rather than Aeneas the Roman, was the ancestor of the people of faith (*fides*), Paul constructs a liberating counter-ideology, the effect of which was to subvert the basis of Roman power. Hence, a conscious consideration of the role of ancestors in

Zimbabwe finds its warrant in Paul's construction of Abraham as a new spiritual ancestor against the background of Roman imperial politics.[3]

This book employs sociohistorical methods to illuminate Paul's creative construction of Abraham as a spiritual ancestor in the Epistle to the Romans, arguing that Romans cannot be understood apart from the imperial age of Augustus. Through the lens of postcolonial biblical interpretation, the project will also seek to demonstrate the colonial and postcolonial reinvention of African Christianity.

Historical and Theological Challenges

Biblical interpretation and exegesis, especially of Paul's letters, must take into consideration people's cultural worldviews, commitments, and experiences. The Augustan revolution, through which Paul's audience lived, was indeed a change in religious, political, and social structures. Cultural interpretation acknowledges that all expressions of Christianity are culturally specific. Similarly, the Roman poet Virgil and the Roman historian Dionysius, on one hand, and the Jewish philosopher Philo and the Jewish historian Josephus, on the other, were all poised to preserve the traditions of their different cultures. Paul, who was a Jew by birth, found himself caught in the contest of the two cultures, and to ignore them would have meant an oversight in his apostleship. So he creatively constructed Abraham in ways that would invite all cultures into the gospel of Jesus Christ. New Testament scholars in the twenty-first century have not yet paid sufficient attention to the intertextuality of Paul's believing audience. In the age of Augustus, religion, power, and politics were inseparable. Paul's ministry was thus confronted with a worldview that required creative approaches.

In many respects, all Christian beliefs, practices, and views of Scripture are embodied or embedded in the interests and dynamics of a particular culture. Culture embodies those moral, ethical, and aesthetic values—the set of spiritual lenses through which people identify both themselves in the universe and their sense of particularity as members of the family of God.[4] On the basis of social-historical investigations of texts, I argue that Paul puts forth a new definition of God for a multiethnic humanity, thus making a postcolonial reading of Romans possible. Paradoxically, Paul depicts Abraham's faith over and against his works, thus engaging Israel's first patriarch in a decidedly new way.[5] In a similar way, Greek and Roman writers of the first century BCE (namely, Dionysius of Halicarnassus, Virgil, and Livy) used Aeneas as a vehicle of Augustan propaganda.

Paul positively and creatively uses the dominant symbols of his day to affirm cultural pluralism and value diversity. Interacting with Mediterranean culture, Paul reinterprets Abraham as the cross-cultural spiritual ancestor of *all* faith people. What Paul does is to counter the dominant theology of the Julio-Claudian family, which was firmly established in the ideology of the ruling elite and the Caesar religion.[6] Thus Paul's appropriation of Abraham as an ancestor of all people suggests to the global community that all traditions can participate in the interpretative process, in which the uniqueness of the other is differentiated, affirmed, and esteemed, while the commonalities of all are identified, shared, and celebrated. In other words, what we find in the Epistle to the Romans is an affirmation of "all" ethnic traditions and an open door for "all" cultures to appropriate the ancestry of Abraham in diversified ways.

As a New Testament theologian, I am concerned with the contextual understanding of Romans and with the cultural construction of the letter's audience in the context of the appropriation of Aeneas as an ancestor of Greeks and Romans. In this regard, the works of Virgil and Dionysius will aid in illumination of Paul's response to the Augustan era. That contextual interpretation will consequently also assist readers to appreciate how the figure of Abraham was adapted and adopted in Africa. As a cross-cultural reader, I recognize the deep need to delineate the complexity of cultural context so that hermeneutical interpretations can be appropriately conveyed as contexts change.

The Aeneas-Abraham paradigm employed in this book is a new discovery born out of my engagement and fascination with the *Aeneid.* In the process of studying the *Aeneid*, I discovered that the connection fits the experiences of African Christians in postcolonial Africa. There is no doubt that the recipients of Paul's Letter to the Romans were familiar with the age of Augustus, especially its ideological stance regarding Aeneas as an ancestor of Greeks and Romans. The language, metaphors, and images Paul uses in Romans were not new to Romans but were present in public buildings in and around their city.[7]

Methodology

Artifacts, coins, images, songs, inscriptions, tombstone epitaphs/poems, and histories from the ancient Greco-Roman and the Mediterranean world are relevant in Pauline commentaries and exegeses. As a postcolonial Bible interpreter, my focus is on bridging the world of the Greco-Roman Empire with the experiences of colonial and postcolonial African Christians. Paul actively appropriates aspects of the *Aeneid* story and makes it central to his Jesus story. That creative action out of a situation of encounter and collision between cultures is a point of solid comparison and analogy between Paul and African experience. Thus a sociohistorical approach is fitting in illuminating the new that was born from the encounter between cultures.

Goal of This Project

Using the Greco-Roman context of ancestors, heroes, and founders, I will situate Paul and his audience within the intertwined religion, politics, and power structures of the Augustan period. The Augustan period was defined by imperial rule, and religion played a sanctioning role in authenticating the ideology of the empire. Religion and control of all life was in many respects the foundation of social dominance by the ruling elite. The purposes of this work are, first, to establish an integration of the ancient Greco-Roman Empire with New Testament interpretations of Paul's theology in Romans and, second and consequently, to assist people in appreciating the complex experiences of African Christians in their encounter with colonialism. The synthesis of colonialism and African culture gave birth to postcolonial Christianity. In this colonial collision and encounter, Africans, like people in the Greco-Roman world, found Paul to be a theological dialogue partner in areas of ancestry, power, and the preservation of identity.

Organization

Chapter 1 is in part autobiographical; it also focuses on the arrival of British missionaries and their perception of African culture. The perception of both colonizers and missionaries is elaborated in order to assist readers to see the complex relationship between Africans and Westerners. European colonialists and missionaries projected themselves as champions of Christian virtue and educators of human values. Their aim then was to educate, evangelize, and produce an African who would be subordinate to the teachings of the Western culture.

Chapter 2 will focus on religious and cultural configurations and an intense engagement between African religion and missionary teachings. In this chapter, colonial and missionary education will be investigated. The study will demonstrate that education, especially "moral and religious education," whether in public or missionary schools, became the incubator of African Christianity.[8]

Chapter 3 identifies postcolonial Christianity in relation to its encounter with Paul, through colonialism, as a theological dialogue partner. Paul's theological argument in Rom. 4:1–25 and the way Africans appropriated and engaged with his message of the gospel of Jesus Christ will be explored as a period not only of synthesis but also of antisynthesis, leading to the birth of an authentic African Christianity. Africans appropriated from Paul's gospel a new understanding of Jesus, of which Paul is the first witness to faith in Jesus Christ.

Chapter 4 will focus on the nature of postcolonial Christianity as African multiethnic Christianity, whose identity is both African and Christian, with a renewed understanding of the role, place, and function of ancestors. Here the study will demonstrate the process and nature of African Shona Christianity's adaptation, faith, and spirituality.

The fifth chapter will offer the argument that the Shona people, in their process of adaptation, already felt an affinity for Paul's idea of ancestry. Here the study will focus on Aeneas and Abraham. The Shona people creatively appropriated selected aspects of Euro-American Christianity in their religion. Paul did the same thing in his Greco-Roman context, and Western New Testament scholars, as those inhabiting the dominant colonial culture, have not seen this adequately. Indeed, the experience of colonization helped Shona Christians to recognize Paul's appropriation of Abraham in the context of the Roman Empire and to counter the ideology of the Julio-Claudian family.

The conclusion summarizes the importance of the Aeneas-Abraham paradigm in the exegesis of Paul's Epistle to the Romans. The comparison between Aeneas and Paul powerfully assists readers to appreciate both Paul's appropriation of the Aeneas story and the ways through which he utilizes it to creatively construct Abraham as a spiritual ancestor, consequently authenticating Christian faith.

This is a powerful theological discovery, for it shows that Paul prefigures exactly what the Shona people did. Paul does not just walk onto the scene arguing for Abraham as an ancestor of Jews, but he selectively appropriates aspects of the *Aeneid* biography and makes it central to his Jesus story. That creative action out of a situation of encounter and collision between cultures is a point of solid comparison and analogy between Paul and Shona Christian experience.

Notes

1. The term *culture* in this work refers to an entire way of life as it pertains to an encounter between Western culture(s) and African traditional religion. Culture encompasses everything that distinguishes one group from others, including social habits and institutions, rituals, artifacts, categorical schemes, beliefs, and values.

2. This particular view is dealt with minimally in Neil Elliot, *The Arrogance of Nations: Reading Romans in the Shadow of the Empire* (Minneapolis: Fortress Press, 2008), 121–38; David R.

Wallace, *The Gospel of God: Rome as Paul's Aenied* (Eugene, OR: Pickwick, 2008), 38–117; and John L. White, *The Apostle of God: Paul and the Promise of Abraham* (Peabody, MA: Hendrickson, 1999), 229–36. My discovery is independent of all these Western New Testament scholars because it is one born from a synthesis and antisynthesis between missionary faith and African indigenous religion. The appropriation of Abraham was in synch with the religious quests in African spirituality and faith.

3. J. R. Harrison, "Paul, Eschatology and the Augustan Age of Grace," *TynBul* 50 (1999): 79–91, offers the same worldview on the encounter between Jewish and Greco-Roman cultures in Rom. 5:12-21 and 8:18-39.

4. Ngugi Wa Thiong'o, *Decolonizing the Mind: The Politics of Language in African Literature* (Nairobi, Kenya: East African Educational Publishers, 1986), 14–15.

5. See Wolfgang Stegemann, "The Emergence of God's New People: The Beginnings of Christianity Reconsidered," *HTS Theological Studies/Teologiese Studies* 62, no. 1 (2006): 23–40 (http://www.hts.org.za/index.php/HTS/article/view/346), who argues that "unlike the many other ancient peoples, the Christianoi as God's people share no common genealogical descent from a common ancestor. Instead, they were connected through fictive kinship, which means that they belong to the household of God (familia dei) and ultimately traced their birth to and from God (baptism as symbolic [re-]birth)" (also published in *Annal di storia dell' esegesis: Come e nato il Cristianesimo?* 21, no. 2 [Centro Italiano di Studi Superiori delle Religioni, 2004]: 497–615). See also Robert Jewett, *Romans: A Commentary*, Hermeneia—A Critical and Historical Commentary on the Bible (Minneapolis: Fortress Press, 2007), 268–322.

6. Dieter Georgi, "Paul" (unpublished manuscript, 2003), 40–41.

7. *Res Gestae* 11.12–13. See P. A. Brunt and J. M. Moore, eds., *Res Gestae Divi Augusti: The Achievements of the Divine Augustus* (Oxford: Oxford University Press, 1967).

8. "Moral and religious education" is used in this book to refer ways cultural imperialism sought to displace and suppress African traditional religion.

1

Empire, Gospel, and Culture

> Colonialism has led to racism, racial discrimination, xenophobia and related intolerance, and . . . Africans and people of African descent, and people of Asian descent and indigenous peoples were victims of colonialism and continue to be victims of its consequences.
>
> - *Durban Declaration of the World Conference against Racism, Racial Discrimination, Xenophobia and Related Intolerance (2001), no. 14, 7.*

To understand a nation, one must look at its history, culture, and religion, as well as the forces that shaped and transformed it. The following brief description of the history and identity of the Shona people of Zimbabwe and their traditional culture is intended to assist readers in understanding the foundations and developments of the Shona people and how they were transformed and shaped first by colonialism and second by missionary encounters. Like the Greeks and Romans, the Shona people have a mythos or a story that is foundational to their community.

Shona Ethnography as Nehanda Mythology

From time immemorial, migration and immigration have shaped and defined human evolution. The Shona people's history is one of migration, conflict, colonial encounters, and reconciliation. Like that of the Greeks and Romans, the Shona story is told and retold because it has significance for one generation after another. Every nation has founders who, in the course of history, have functioned as ancestors, religious priests, or political pillars. The foundations of the Shona can easily be traced to an area south of Zimbabwe called Masvingo, to an ancient city known as "Great Zimbabwe."[1] There is no doubt that Great Zimbabwe is the nerve center of Shona religion, politics, economics, and social life. By the eleventh century CE, there was at Great Zimbabwe a powerful and organized trading society founded by the Shona ancestors.

Although Great Zimbabwe is no longer the center of the Shona worldview, the ruined city remains part of Shona foundational legend. Hence, the place is now called "Zimbabwean Ruins," uninhabited but preserved as a valuable cultural center and tourist attraction. The place is attractive because of its stone walls that continue to stand even in the twenty-first century. European explorers and missionaries called one ruined edifice the "Acropolis and the Temple," because it has a number of enclosures that lead into the inner religious parts of the complex. The name Zimbabwe is derived from these massive impressive stone walls, called *dzimba dzamambwe*, which in Shona means "stone buildings."

God, kings, and Shona spirits were believed to reside in this place; even today people call it "the dwelling place of gods and kings." Historical and archaeological discoveries have confirmed that in 1903, Great Zimbabwe was a center of much trade with nations such as India, China, and Persia, as well as the Near East and the Middle East. It is crucial to recognize that the people of Great Zimbabwe were involved not only in local trade but in international trade as well. The contact with other nationalities will be considered in the section below discussing missionary encounters, especially regarding the reception of the Abrahamic faith. Here it suffices to note that before the arrival of the British, Shona culture had contact with people from various parts of the world.

Notable artifacts that include huge soapstone birds have been discovered at Great Zimbabwe; these birds played a significant role in Shona religious culture. The bird, known in Shona as *Shiri ya Mwari, Hungwe Shirichena*, or God's bird of white plumage, was familiar in and around Great Zimbabwe. Religiously, the bird's function was to interpret the voice of God. Spirit mediums were able to understand and explain what God was saying through this bird, and, in most cases, the bird was rewarded with gifts of fruit and drink.[2] If this was the case, one can safely say that Great Zimbabwe was the epicenter of Shona religion and culture, and possibly the spiritual headquarters of the Shona ancestral cosmology.

Among other functions, Great Zimbabwe served as a military and economic center because of its location on the edge of the major gold-producing areas of southwestern Zimbabwe. Therefore, it is possible that a combination of religious, economic, and military factors contributed to political and administrative centralization by Shona kings and rulers. The power of kings was consolidated both by economic interests and religious institutions situated in Great Zimbabwe between centers of production (toward the west) and marketing (toward the coast on the east). At the height of its glory and greatness, Great Zimbabwe attracted people from all over Africa, including Swahili-speaking people from the east coast of Africa. Great Zimbabwe was a place not only of trade, religion, and economics but also of political conflicts among ethnic rulers.

Shona history suggests that the decline of Great Zimbabwe was due to shortages of salt, a common commodity for cooking. I propose a more nuanced reason for decline. While salt is central in Shona traditions, it is also a symbol of wealth and prosperity. Thus, when Shona traditions mention the shortage of salt at Great Zimbabwe, it means that there was a great shortage of food supplies, pastures, fuel, gold, and copper not only at Great Zimbabwe but also around the city's hinterland. The scarcity of natural resources at Great Zimbabwe gave birth to new Shona ethnic empires, ruled by Mutota, who was the chief architect of the Changamire Empire, the Mwenemutapa Empire in the northern part of Zimbabwe, and the Rozvi Empire and Matopo Hills in Matabeleland. As the ruler of these empires, Mutota was always in search of better areas in and around Great Zimbabwe.

By the late fifteenth century, Great Zimbabwe faced competition from Shona ethnic dynasties in and around the region. The three main rivers in Zimbabwe—Mazoe, Zambezi, and Limpopo—were significant components of the Shona economy. The Mazoe River, a major tributary of the Zambezi River, linked the Zimbabwean goldfields and heartland with lower Zambezi trading settlements. The Mwenemutapa Empire also established trade routes to full capacity, linking all three major rivers. Thus, when David Livingstone and Cecil John Rhodes came to Zimbabwe in the mid-nineteenth century, they found these trading routes in place and exploited them to their advantage.

Other stone walls were erected in and around Zimbabwe, each imitating the complexity of Great Zimbabwe. Nonetheless, Great Zimbabwe still remains the birthplace of Shona religion, politics, and economics and continues to function today as a historic religious, cultural, and tourist center. Great Zimbabwe will always be a place of religious significance, as well as the spiritual headquarters of the Shona ancestors. Colonial and postcolonial Shona Christianity has to an extent been formed and shaped by the religious symbols of Great Zimbabwe. When explorers and missionaries came to Zimbabwe, they found local leaders already practicing African religion and participating in trade. It is to this that I now turn.

David Livingstone and Cecil John Rhodes

Although the Portuguese were the first to arrive in Zimbabwe, the Englishmen Livingstone and Rhodes occupy a major place in the exploration and evangelization of Africa, especially Zimbabwe. The two foreshadowed the colonization and missionary enterprise in and around Zimbabwe. David Livingstone came to Africa as an explorer under the leadership of Dr. Robert Moffat in 1841 and established a number of mission centers in and around Zimbabwe. In his travels within Zimbabwe, Livingstone was impressed by great rivers, which he thought were navigable on which he sought to reach the heart of Africa. After discovering the great rivers, Livingstone abandoned his missionary activities and carried out a period of geographical discovery and exploration. Between 1849 and 1851, Livingstone devoted all his time to the exploration of Africa, and he made three major expeditions in and around Zimbabwe.

In 1852, Livingstone started his first expedition that saw him in Matabeleland, where he entered into a partnership with King Kololo of the Bulozi tribe. The exploration brought Livingstone to the Zambezi River, where, for the first time, he saw the most spectacular waterfall of the river, exemplified by his renaming what would be hailed as one of the seven wonders of the world from its original Shona name of *Mosi-o-tunya*, or "the smoke that thunders," to Victoria Falls, in honor of his queen.[3] The plateaus in and around the falls were so impressive that Livingstone decided to establish European settlements and Christian missions there. After his first expedition, Livingstone returned to England, where he received a hero's welcome and made presentations to the British public.[4] He made an appeal to all the British people to consider Zimbabwe as a viable mission field.

Livingstone also extended special appeals to businesspeople to open up trade in Africa. His dream was to open a path to commerce and Christianity. In 1856, Livingstone again returned to England. His findings on Zimbabwe were published in *Missionary Travels and Researches in South Africa*, and more than twelve thousand copies were sold.[5] He gave a number of presentations to British libraries and universities as well as to British Parliament. His presentations to British audiences were so successful with both the public and the government in that the British government sponsored his second expedition.

In his farewell speech from England, Livingstone said, "I go back to Central Africa to try to open up a path to commerce and Christianity. Do you carry out the work that I have begun? I leave it up to you!" Inspired by these words, British business entrepreneurs, traders, and missionaries provided

Livingstone and his team with boats and a steamer to sail the rivers of central Africa.

The expedition arrived in Zimbabwe in March 1858 and began to explore the region. The group established relationships with African rulers, African traditional religious leaders, and local people. These relations led to the occupation, colonization, and evangelization of Zimbabwe. By 1866, most parts of Zimbabwe had been reached by British explorers and missionaries. On May 1, 1873, Livingstone died, and his body was shipped to England, where he was buried at Westminster Abbey in London.[6]

While Livingstone died without experiencing the fruit of his labors and dreams for Africa, he indeed was the harbinger of colonization and missionary work in Zimbabwe. His failures as a missionary were probably because he did not see his role as one of building mission stations and converting local people to Christianity. His main objective was to open African frontiers to British colonizers and missionaries. He was indeed the greatest explorer of Africa in the nineteenth century. His observations about the peoples of Zimbabwe, their beliefs, customs, and traditions—often restricted by his Victorian and Christian views—are fundamental to understanding the encounters between African and Western cultures.

Clearly, Livingstone was eager to leave the practical work of establishing mission centers and converting people to Christianity to those who felt called by God. As a founder of European colonization, Livingstone appealed not only to Christian agents to come to Zimbabwe but also to European businessmen and farmers to settle, occupy, and colonize Shona cultures. This was because he believed that only Christianity, European commerce, and development could bring an end to slave trade, tribal conflicts, and, consequently, transformation of the Shona worldview. Whether Livingstone would have agreed on the manner in which Zimbabwe was later colonized and evangelized, the point is that he opened doors to both pioneer Christian missionaries and colonizers.

Cecil John Rhodes: The Pioneer Colonizer of Zimbabwe

I do not intend to rewrite the history of Cecil John Rhodes and his occupation of Zimbabwe, but I nevertheless offer a brief analysis of the central role he played in both colonization and mission work in Zimbabwe.[7] Inspired by Livingstone's writings on Africa, Rhodes went to South Africa in 1868 to join his brother, who had already started a cotton farm there. The years between 1868 and 1871 saw the discovery of diamonds in South Africa. Rhodes, who had joined diamond diggers, used his shrewd British business skills to establish several profitable business ventures, including the famous De Beers Mining

Company, becoming a millionaire in the process. With money in hand, Rhodes sought to gain power by spreading British imperialistic principles. He was a strong believer in British superiority, its systems of government and justice, and its principles of peace and liberty. Rhodes was an arrogant advocate of British imperialism and was prepared to spend his fortune spreading British principles in and around Zimbabwe, and he wanted Britain to occupy the rest of Africa. His aims for and dreams of a vast African empire resulted in his being labeled the biggest empire builder of the nineteenth century. In this respect, he was like the Romans and Greeks, whose ideals and mores were enshrined in Aeneas.

By 1884, Africa was a battleground of Western imperialism, with every European country seeking to colonize and occupy a place within the continent. As a shrewd businessman and colonizer, Rhodes persuaded the British government to make missionary roads secure by establishing colonies and by declaring protectorates in southern and central Africa. In 1887, Rhodes, with the help of the British high commissioner, signed a treaty with King Lobengula of the Ndebele people, the second largest tribe in Zimbabwe. Under the treaty, Lobengula agreed to befriend the British queen and promised not to enter into any agreement with another nation without the knowledge and approval of the British high commissioner. With this agreement, part of Zimbabwe became a part of the British Empire.

The illiterate king did not fully understand what he had done to his own land and people. While he regarded Rhodes and other white people as friends, Lobengula's tribe began to experience an influx of British visitors into their land. These British citizens had one aim in mind: to colonize and mine gold in and around Zimbabwe. Under false pretense, the British acted as good friends and persuaded Lobengula to sign more treaties, which granted British groups further mining and trading concessions, and in return the British would help to defend the region from other nations. Rhodes used his personal fortune to secure his strong political position in Zimbabwe, to the extent that he even undermined the queen of England. He also had substantial influence among some leading personalities in both Zimbabwe and Britain. He owned millions of pounds of the De Beers money from Cape Town, which he used to buy or bribe rivals and opponents in southern Africa and Britain.

Rhodes's next move was to form a partnership with the British South African Company with the hope of finally colonizing the rest of Zimbabwe and exploiting its mineral and other resources. After he formed this partnership, in 1889, the British South African Company became a force of change in Zimbabwe. The company needed a royal charter from the queen of England, to authorize their having absolute power over the people of Zimbabwe. After months of negotiation, the charter was given, which consequently led to the colonization of Zimbabwe. King Lobengula of the Ndebele was greatly undermined by the royal charter, and the rest of the region was now under the control of Rhodes, who began to recruit well-trained artisans and young traders from England.

The recruited skilled people, who became the British Pioneer Column, included blacksmiths, carpenters, builders, printers, bakers, miners, farmers, and traders. Each of these people was promised three thousand acres of land on arrival in Mashonaland territory and up to fifteen gold claims. In September 1890, the British Pioneer Column made their settlement at a place the leaders called Fort Salisbury, in honor of the imperialist British prime minister. It was clear to the Ndebele and Shona kings and their subjects that the whites had come not only to trade or to look for gold but also to settle, conquer, occupy, and rule the entire region of Zimbabwe.

The years between 1890 and 1980 were characterized by nearly a century of wars, uprisings, evangelism, and complete domination of Zimbabwe by the British. The Shona became a source of cheap labor and were mistakenly regarded as cowards by the British colonizers. With white administration at the center of Shona culture, Rhodes took a final step of renaming Zimbabwe. In 1895, Zimbabwe was colonially and officially renamed Rhodesia, in honor of Rhodes, who claimed to be the founder of a new nation. Having successfully claimed Zimbabwe, Rhodes divided the region into two main administrative provinces: Mashonaland (eastern Zimbabwe) and Matabeleland (western Zimbabwe). British colonization brought not only administrative change of territorial divisions but also forced labor, forced taxation, cultural change, and religious change, among other things. Highways and cities were given British names, political oppression was the order of the day, and the best land was freely given to the British settlers. Missions, schools, and hospitals were introduced and functioned for the most part as preparatory centers for training African minds to be subject to colonial and missionary agendas. Colonialists were eager to offer a form of education to blacks that would transform them to serve colonial masters.[8]

It became clear to both the Ndebele and Shona people that Rhodes had come to colonize, conquer, and transform the Shona worldview. Both the Ndebele and Shona people lost their cattle and land to Rhodes, who by 1895 had introduced white administration to the entire region. The British government promoted many injustices and cared little for the people whose land they colonized and whose culture they disregarded as heathenism. This made the Shona people very bitter and incited them to resist white rule in Zimbabwe.

Determined to fight for their land, religious leaders from both the Ndebele and Shona responded by conducting uprisings against British occupation of Zimbabwe. In both eastern and western Zimbabwe, whites were targeted and, within weeks, about one hundred white families were killed. The response from Rhodes was brutal and furious: he declared war on the indigenous people. While whites had the advantage of superior weapons, the Shona people had bows and arrows, Mwari (God), and ancestors on their side.

Shona Ancestors and Their Appeal to Mwari

Two fundamental factors are worth noting. First, from time immemorial, Zimbabwe was composed of many tribal entities, united religiously and culturally by a strong belief in God, who in native language was referred to as Mwari. The monotheism and spirituality of the indigenous people were obvious to the British missionaries who arrived in the 1890s. In Shona society, God was known by many names or appellations and was approached through intermediaries whom the Shona venerated as ancestors. Among the Ndebele people, God was worshiped at the Matopo Hills near present-day Bulawayo. Among the Shona people in eastern Zimbabwe, Mwari was worshiped in every chiefdom and village.

Second, ancestors, regarded as founders of a nation, were highly esteemed; in the worldview of the Shona people, ancestors occupied a central role. They were not worshiped in African culture; rather they were considered as founders and spiritual agents whose role is to communicate the message of God to the people. Often, they were a means to reconciliation between tribes and conflicting parties.

For purposes of this book, I will concentrate mainly on one Shona ancestor named Nehanda, who has received little attention, yet played a pivotal role during the colonial period and years of liberation wars.

In the late nineteenth century, Nehanda Charwe Nyakasikane (c. 1840–1898) was considered to possess supernatural powers. She was imbued with a direct connection to deity analogous to that attributed to the ancestors of Greeks and Romans.[9] Her role and place in Shona religion and culture resonated with core Shona beliefs in such a way that she captured the worldview of her people by persuading them that Mwari was against the British colonization of Zimbabwe. She encouraged the Shona chiefs and political leaders to expel the British from Zimbabwe. Though her role was prominent throughout the British incursion, it was especially so in 1896, when the Ndebele and Shona tribes joined forces in resisting white occupation. Through her spiritual powers, she convinced nationalistic leaders that whites were responsible for all the suffering and natural disasters that engulfed the nation. Before Nehanda's influence, natural disasters meant only one thing to the Shona people—an expression of God's anger.

The uprisings (1896–1897) against the colonialists were inevitable because the colonial occupation had seriously undermined Shona religion, culture, and political independence. Nehanda's role in multiple wars of liberation was prominent, and she was considered to be the female incarnation of the oracle spirit grandmother of the Shona people. Nehanda decreed that whites must be driven by force from Zimbabwe, and she summoned other religious leaders to join her in the resistance. Thus religious leaders in both eastern and western Zimbabwe joined in the war of resistance. Religious and ancestral leaders such as Nehanda gave religious sanction to the risings and used their religious places as command centers for intelligence purposes. The development of the Mwari cult from 1896 to 1897 led to the establishment of cults all over the country, so much so that political leaders and ancestral spirits collaborated in training and sending young warriors to fight the British. Through use of secret messages to communicate with other spirit mediums, she effectively coordinated a powerful resistance force.

The British tried to persuade religious leaders to join them and even at times bribed them to accept British occupation, but Nehanda resisted. Her spiritual powers and influence were indeed behind the birth of postcolonial Zimbabwe. She finally became a target of the British and was captured in 1897. She was sentenced to death by hanging in 1898, to the end steadfastly refusing and denouncing British occupation of Zimbabwe.

In her dying words, Nehanda told the British, "My bones will rise again." These few words were a source of inspiration to the second generation of liberation fighters, and were finally realized in the war that culminated in the independence of Zimbabwe in 1980, when her remains were given a heroine's burial at Zimbabwe's Heroes' Acre, a memorial place for all who fought for the independence of the Shona and Ndebele people. Her role in resisting British colonization qualifies her to be the founder of the Shona people.

The spirit of Nehanda did not die with her hanging; rather, it appeared in other female religious leaders, who were constantly consulted on military decisions during the war of liberation. The spirit of Nehanda and her prophecies provided valuable assistance to the revolutionary struggle and rebirth of postcolonial Zimbabwe. Female leaders who were possessed with Nehanda's spirit were always in conflict with colonization, so much so that during the second war of liberation, British settlers sought to kill them. In 1972, the spirit of Nehanda found a new medium in an elderly woman who was eventually taken to Mozambique by freedom fighters. While in exile, she continued to be a source of inspiration and guidance to the operations of Shona people in Zimbabwe. Thus religious leaders and spirit mediums were the revolutionary forces that brought an end to British occupation.

I contend that Shona people can be called Nehanda people because their political, social, and religious foundations are shaped and informed by the indomitable spirit and revolutionary prophetic stance of Nehanda, a female spiritual leader who resisted the imposition of British colonialism, which finally led to a postcolonial Zimbabwe in 1980. As a New Testament scholar from the Shona diaspora, I do not intend to speak on behalf of all the Shona people, however, nor do I suggest that their cultural theology has not changed.

What I seek to offer is an African hermeneutical perspective that can help both Western and African Christian theologians appropriate a cultural, theological understanding of the apostle Paul and his creative reshaping of Abraham in the book of Romans. In his essay "The Case for a New Bible," Canaan Banana, a British Methodist clergyman, argues, "The people in the Bible—both Old and New Testament—are people whose lives and faith response to God provide lessons for who come after. Each culture has its record of those people."[10] Banana is right: Zimbabweans have such figures as *Mbuya*, or Grandmother Nehanda, and other traditional religious leaders whose lives opened new possibilities for postcolonial Shona culture.

Nehanda, as a founder of the Shona people, fought relentlessly to defend her people's religious, cultural, and political values against adulteration by Western colonizers. She died a martyr at the hands of British overlords on account of her religious convictions.[11] Her indomitable courage was immortalized in the hearts and minds of young, gallant Zimbabwean fighters for African heritage.[12] Thus Nehanda is venerated in present-day Zimbabwe as the spiritual founder of a postcolonial Zimbabwe.

Her status is similar to that of Aeneas (and of Abraham), and she must be accorded an honored place alongside such leading religious leaders from other ancient cultures. Virgil, as well as the poet of the *Odyssey* and *Iliad*, celebrates Aeneas as the founding father of Greeks and Romans. Virgil's *Aeneid* documents the tale of pious Aeneas, ancestor of the house of Caesar, leading his people and his gods from fallen Troy to the land of the Romans.[13] Both Homer and Virgil represent a literary culture at its most authoritative. Their stories were learned by many in and around the Greco-Roman Empire, stamped on the memory of every literate person. The ideology they sought to transmit defines much of what the world knows as of the Greco-Romans Empire.

In similar manner, Nehanda's story is engraved in the hearts and memories of Shona people, and her struggles with European colonizers define much of what the world knows of Zimbabwe. Her struggles against colonization are a fitting hermeneutic for biblical interpretation in Zimbabwe because her story resembles that of faith-founders such as Abraham. As a contemporary Shona Christian, I seek to offer an autobiographical experience of the colonial and missionary presence in Zimbabwe, as well as the aftermath of this encounter. The primary theological challenge most Shona people face involves maintaining a balance between being an African and being a Christian. In spite of its adverse effects, colonization and missionary enterprises in Zimbabwe initiated for the Shona an era of both progress and change. The preservation of Shona ancestral culture and the adaptation of traditional institutions to meet Christian innovations is the principal theme of this book.

Nature and Identity of the Shona or Nehanda People

The Shona, who are rightly called Nehanda people, are not a people without myths. Like Greeks, Romans, and Jews, they too have stories to tell about their gods, ancestors, and the achievements of their nation. The Shona were indeed profoundly influenced by British and American ideas and ideals in politics, religion, and social life. The culture known as "Shona" originated from a Bantu settlement of the high fertile plateau between the Limpopo and Zambezi Rivers, bounded in the east by the Kalahari Desert.[14] The Shona of Zimbabwe refer to persons as *munhu* (singular) and *vanhu* (plural). Etymologically, the term *Bantu/Vanhu* simply refers to human beings who inhabit central and southern Africa. Modern inhabitants of Zimbabwe still refer to themselves as descendants of Bantu: simply meaning people or human beings.

By the end of the second century BCE, the first Bantu migration from the north settled in what is now Zimbabwe, and they had great allegiance to ancestors.[15] Among these migrant groups were bands of stone-age Khoisan migrants, commonly known as the Bushmen. The ancestors of the Bantu migrated in search of pasture lands, good agricultural areas, water, and stock-raising areas. One important legacy of the Bantu-speaking peoples is that they linguistically borrowed from each other and were physically integrated. They finally settled in what is now called central and southern Africa. In contemporary Zimbabwe, Bantu people are classified into five ethnic categories, namely, "the *Zezuru*, *Korekore*, *Karanga*, *Manyika*, and *Ndau* people."[16] Shona peoples did not call themselves by this name, but the extension of the term to all ethnic tribes in Zimbabwe appears to have been a British colonial innovation.

The other largest ethnic group of people in Zimbabwe is the Ndebele, who in the third century BCE migrated from South Africa to settle in an area called Bulawayo. It is believed that they were from the tribe of Soshangane, who was a Zulu king in the eastern part of South Africa.[17] The Ndebele arrived with the powerful military organization developed by the Zulu and were able to conduct raids deep into the Shona areas, collecting women and cattle from defeated peoples. Nevertheless, the Ndebele and the Shona were able to live together as different people, with their own ancestors, cultural values, and political differences. The autochthonous Shona peoples were able to maintain their autonomy against various outside influences, to the extent that they became the official largest ethnic group in Zimbabwe.

Shona became the language of communication, followed by the Ndebele language and other tribal languages in and around Zimbabwe. Politically and linguistically, Zimbabwe has two major regions, categorized as Mashonaland and Matabeleland, with the former predominantly speaking the Shona language as well as other dialects. The latter speaks what is called Ndebele, which is basically the Zulu language. Thus Shona contemporary groupings cover most of Zimbabwe, with ethnic peoples within the region speaking different dialects. Independent chiefdoms, united by geographical propinquity and their common Shona language, culture, and religious affiliation, define the people of Zimbabwe and give them a sense of distinctiveness.

Indeed, by the time British colonialists and American missionaries arrived, African religion was already well developed and was practiced by the major ethnic groups in Zimbabwe, including the Ndebele people. By 1890, Zimbabwe was united religiously by a strong belief in *Mwari/Mwali* (God), whom the Shona religious priests and followers called the Supreme Being. Both missionaries and colonialists viewed the Mwari cult, or God cult, with great suspicion. The home of the cult of the High God, Mwali or Mwari, was centered in the Matopo Hills of Bulawayo.[18] While the Ndebele and Shona lived together and worshiped the same God, they had different political, religious, and cultural heroes whom they venerated as spirit mediums able to hear from Mwari and to transmit the message to all peoples. These spirit mediums were known as Mhondoro and founders of a people.

The Shona had great reverence for three major figures—namely, Nehanda, Chaminuka, and Kaguvi—with Nehanda, the female spirit medium described above, being given a prominent role. The Ndebele people had great reverence for Mzilikazi. The outbreak of the risings in both western and eastern

Zimbabwe and the campaigns of resistance by both the Ndebele and the Shona were to a large extent attributable to the working relationship between the Mhondoro cults and Mwari. The history of Shona Christianity in Zimbabwe is a complex and intriguing compound of romance, idealism, courage, arrogance, association, avarice, and construction. By 1870, most of Zimbabwe had had an encounter with both European and American cultural agents, who had different interests. The Europeans were interested in hunting, trading, exploration, and the colonization of Zimbabwe. On the contrary, Americans were well invested in missionary work, evangelism, and farming. They established health facilities, educational centers, and theological centers that later became incubators of African Christianity during and after the colonial era. Moreover, Shona Christianity involved, on a larger scale, intractable problems similar to those faced by the apostle Paul in his Greco-Roman missionary world, namely, power dynamics among nationalities, Roman ideology, ancestral claims, religious mores, and Christian faith. While Aeneas and Abraham were competing ancestors in the Greco-Roman world, the British Empire, represented by Cecil John Rhodes, competed with indigenous culture with its allegiance to ancestors and Christian missionaries. Thus the synthesis and antithesis of the colonial encounter with indigenous culture greatly transformed the future of postcolonial indigenous Christianity.

Zimbabwe was, in fact, a great deal more primitive for both colonizers and missionaries, at least from the perspective of Western imperialism. They both aspired to bring civilization and light to a people whose culture they considered superstitious, backward, and heathen. The goal of the colonists and missionaries was threefold—to civilize, evangelize, and colonize. They introduced a way of life that was first and foremost European and North American, stamped with Western Christianity. The man who came to embody this new ethos of empire was David Livingstone, a champion of both missionary and colonial domination of Zimbabwe.[19] The institution that embodied evangelism was the London Missionary Society (LMS) under the leadership of John Smith Moffat.[20] For Livingstone, commerce and colonization—the original foundations of the empire—were necessary but not sufficient.

By allusion and analogy, Nehanda, who came to embody resistance against the Europeans, became a new Abraham, who through her valor embodied the religious, political, and cultural framework of Zimbabweans. Nehanda's goal was to resist foreign domination, but her efforts met with imperial ideologies of self-aggrandizement. I turn next to discuss the complexities of the postcolonial situation for Zimbabwean communities, including their encounters with the colonists and missionaries. For some, the encounter was one of resistance, compromise, or cultural renaissance.

Scramble, Conquest, Mission, and Colonization of Zimbabwe

It is no exaggeration to say that by the mid-1870s, central Africa had encountered European imperialism. Overpopulation and land hunger in Europe, opportunities for commerce, trading, social advancement abroad, exploration, and evangelism are some of the well-documented claims that led to the colonization of Africa, especially Zimbabwe. While few African or European leaders failed to see the revolutionary changes that would come to Zimbabwe, *Mbuya*, or Grandmother Nehanda, the spirit medium of Zimbabwe, sternly warned indigenous people of the encroachment of white settlers. The results of her prophetic predictions were experienced within a matter of months, if not weeks. The Berlin Conference, to regulate European colonization and trade in Africa, took place in 1884–1885 and laid the foundation for what is called the scramble for Africa or partition of Africa.[21] The seeds of colonial and missionary ventures were sown at this meeting, which resulted in the General Act of the conference at Berlin. The act laid geographical boundaries in Africa for the various European imperial powers, leading to an influx of Western missionaries and colonialists to partition Africa without regard to native cultures or languages.

The partition of Africa led to the invasion, occupation, and annexation of African land by such people as Cecil John Rhodes. While Rhodes is credited as the vanguard of imperialism, his arrival in Zimbabwe did not precede that of missionaries. African theologians, historians, and politicians have for years argued that colonialism and Christianity came to Zimbabwe at the same time. I contend that Christian missionaries were the first to set foot in Zimbabwe in 1829 and thus paved the way for colonialists.[22] By 1829, British and Portuguese Christian missionaries had visited three main countries: Zimbabwe, Zambia, and Malawi. In the fifteenth century, the Portuguese missionaries had been the first to evangelize central Africa, but their efforts did not produce any converts. Under the leadership of Dr. Robert Moffat, a Scottish missionary, the Portuguese missions came under the banner of the London Missionary Society and established relations with Mzilikazi, the Ndebele king.

Through friendships with local kings and leaders, missionaries were allowed to establish mission centers and devoted most of their time and energy to teaching, preaching, and literacy work. With the passing of time, books and Bibles in indigenous languages were printed first in Bulawayo and then in Harare. The medium through which literacy and the Western worldview were transmitted to indigenous people was colonial and missionary education. Chapter 2 will focus on the role colonial and missionary education played in forming, shaping, and awakening Shona religious worldview through the reconstruction and appropriation of Paul's theology.

Notes

1. D. E. Nedham, E. K. Mashingaidze, and N. Bhebhe, eds., *From Iron Age to Independence: A History of Central Africa* (Harare, Zimbabwe: Longman, 1984), 15.

2. The bird is depicted today on most Zimbabwean coins and even on notes.

3. David Livingstone was the most well-known European missionary-explorer of central Africa and the first one to be fascinated by the Victoria Falls, but he was by no means the only European to set foot on the continent; there where others before him such as the Portuguese, who penetrated central Africa from Mozambique. Robert Moffat of the London Missionary Society was also before David Livingstone.

4. See Needham, Mashingaidze, and Bhebe, eds., *From Iron Age to Independence*, 90–92.

5. David Livingstone, *Missionary Travels and Researches in South Africa* (London, 1857). This work is also available online at http://www.gutenberg.org/files/1039/1039-h/1039-h.htm, and in various modern print and ebook formats.

6. Needham, Mashingaidze, and Bhebe, eds., *From Iron Age to Independence*, 46.

7. Cecil John Rhodes's history is well documented in ibid., 111–21.

8. Ethel Tawse Jolie, who was elected to the Rhodesian Legislative Council in 1920, argued, "We do not intend to hand over this country to the Natives. Let us make no pretense of educating them in the same way we educate Whites." Dickson A. Mungazi, *Colonial Education for Africans: George Stark's Policy in Zimbabwe* (New York: Praeger, 1991), 1.

9. See T. P. Wisemann, *The Myths of Rome* (Devon, UK: University of Exeter Press, 2004). Wiseman helps readers to understand the *Aeneid* story as a legendary poem of Greek and Roman founders whose stories were evolving from oral cultures to literate times. At the center of these stories is the prominent role of Aeneas, who wandered from the land of the Molossians and joined with Odysseus in founding Rome. Similarly, Nehanda of Zimbabwe is not just a mythical figure but a real female ancestress heroine whose story helps to identify and signify the identity, ethos, and mores of the Shona people.

10. Canaan S. Banana, *Rewriting the Bible: The Real Issues* (Gweru, Zimbabwe: Mambo Press, 1993), 17–32.

11. Ibid.

12. Ibid.

13. For a detailed discussion of Aeneas, see Wiseman, *The Myths of Rome*, 215–16.

14. The word *Bantu* is used in this book to simply mean the largest ethnic peoples or human beings who settled in central Africa in the second century BCE and their contemporary descendants. For an elaborate history of the Bantu people, see Needham, Mashingaidze, and Bhebe, eds., *From Iron Age to Independence*, 5–14.

15. M. F. C. Bourdillion, *The Shona Peoples: An Ethnography of the Contemporary Shona, with Special Reference to Their Religion* (Harare, Zimbabwe: Mambo Press, 1987), 6–7.

16. Ibid., 16–17.

17. Ibid., 14.

18. Terence Ranger, *Voices from the Rocks: Nature, Culture and History in the Matopos Hills of Zimbabwe* (Bloomington: Indiana University Press, 1999), 11–38.

19. See Musa Dube, *Postcolonial Feminist Interpretation of the Bible* (St. Louis: Chalice, 2000), 5–6.

20. See Needham, Mashingaidze, and Bhebe, eds., *From Iron Age to Independence*, 96–101.

21. Represented at the Berlin Conference were Austria-Hungary, Belgium, Denmark, France, Germany, Great Britain, Italy, the Netherlands, Portugal, Russia, Spain, Sweden-Norway, Turkey, and the United States. France, Germany, Great Britain, and Portugal were the major players in the conference.

22. Needham, Mashingaidze, and Bhebe, eds., *From Iron Age to Independence*, 96.

2

Zimbabwe's Religious Cultural Configurations

Father Abraham had many sons
Many sons had Father Abraham
I am one of them and so are you
So let's all praise the Lord!

The period of colonial expansion and missionary education saw the transformation of Shona religion, culture, identity, and social structures. From the beginning, the educational process of both Africans and whites was the responsibility of colonial administrators and missionaries. When Western Christian missionaries came to Zimbabwe, their two main objectives were to supplant African traditional religion with Christianity and to civilize the so-called pagan natives of the Dark Continent.[1] They sought to do this through moral and religious education, which in the Christian sense included all efforts and processes that help to bring children and adults into a vital and saving experience of God revealed in Jesus Christ. Religious education, whether in government or mission schools, was also meant to quicken the sense of God as a living reality so that communion with God became a natural practice and principle of life. The avenue to achieve all this was through Bible recitation, music, catechism, drama, and memorized Bible passages.

This perception of and approach to Christianity by missionaries shaped and formed Shona Christianity in both colonial and postcolonial times. Caught in this empirical scenario, Shona religion was confronted with an either-or situation. Notwithstanding the force of the European empire, Shona people were drawn to elements of what the missionaries had to offer. A major factor that forged links between the Shona people and missionaries was the establishment of strategic centers around Zimbabwe. These mission centers were composed of elementary and high school education, hospitals, farms, and theological education,[2] which attracted Shona religious leaders, including chiefs and tribal leaders—an attraction they valued, appropriated, and, eventually, Africanized. However, colonial masters took over ownership of land and natural resources and stripped chiefs of their power.

The question at the center of this confrontation was: How is African traditional religion to be preserved? The answer determined the ways through which the Shona people would navigate both the missionary and colonial worldviews. On the one hand, the Shona people held to a desire to preserve their African traditional religion. On the other hand, missionary education presented the Shona with an opportunity to transmute and transform their religious experience, along with other opportunities for personal, social, and community development. How then would the Shona people respond to missionary Christianity without despising their own traditional religion? How would Shona people use missionary education as a resource for dealing with colonialism? Keeping this dichotomy in perspective, this chapter will examine the impact of missionary education during and after colonization.

While this chapter offers an original and provocative interpretation of the changes brought about by colonial and missionary education, it also documents a well-planned effort by missionaries to place mission centers in vital areas of Zimbabwe.

The aim of these mission centers was to target and reclaim the total worldview of the Africans. On arrival in Zimbabwe, missionaries planted mission stations that served two major purposes. First, mission centers were religious sanctuaries designed to protect the missionaries from local people. More importantly, these centers later developed into institutions for education, health care, farming, and evangelism.[3] Indigenous people—especially women, who were persecuted within the culture—found mission centers to be places of refuge where they found sympathy and protection from harsh traditional customs.[4] Whether mission centers fulfilled their intended purposes is an issue to keep in mind as this book unfolds.

My thesis is that mission centers were incubators of cultural and religious change, change that would later transform Shona social structures and ways of religious practice. At the center of this change was the Bible, a book whose reading and interpretation was presented by two groups of "missionaries": Victorian colonizers, on the one hand, figures such as Cecil John Rhodes and David Livingstone, who sought to carry out a "civilizing" *cultural* mission and thus promoted colonial policies of subjugating the Africans;[5] and Christian missionaries, on the other hand, who had as their primary objective converting Africans to Christianity.

Philosophically, both groups based their education on the same principle: the only form of education from which Africans could benefit was manual labor and practical training. The underlying rationale for this belief was that Africans could more readily acquire basic elements of Western civilization by imitating whites and performing practical and readily applicable tasks than by any other means. In order to understand why both groups pursued the policies they did, it is important to understand the context in which those policies were formulated. Westerners did not believe Africans were less than human but were convinced that they possessed an intellect decidedly inferior to that of whites. This was a major component of both Victorian colonizers and Christian missionaries, and they both operated according to that philosophy. Thus the Bible was used as a textbook in a classroom setting for literacy training and as a holy book for religious instruction, Christian catechism, and church preaching.

Four major changes happened as a result of this approach: new opportunities for literacy, African perception of the character of the Western missionary, the psychology of the colonial government officials, and the rise of African consciousness in areas of religion, faith, and spirituality. I will discuss each change to show how it gave birth to Shona multiethnic Christianity.

First, literacy, or the ability to read the English Bible, gave Africans new forms of knowledge. Teachers presented factual events and verbal order with one goal in mind: to help students pass a biblical examination. Both students and teachers worked successfully in obtaining good grades because the students memorized facts and portions of Scripture. But this was not by any means moral and religious education. Teachers were inclined to impart information without helping students develop clear insights and attitudes that reflected the meaning of the Bible.

Second, when Christian missionaries persuaded Africans to embrace the ideals of Christianity, they were in essence asking them to discard their own culture as a condition of acceptance into the Christian community. In failing to appreciate the positive attributes of African culture, the missionaries made it hard for the two cultural groups to create the environment that promoted an understanding of biblical Christianity. If missionaries had understood the religious context of Africans, they would have designed a strategy different from the one they pursued. Methodist Bishop Ralph Dodge, who served as a missionary to Africa from 1936 to 1972, discussed the negative impact of Victorian missionaries on the colonization of Africa when he wrote, "The participation of the Church in the slave trade and its unwillingness at critical times to identify itself with the indigenous people, made it often considered a European colonial institution. This situation was accentuated by close identification of the Church with European colonial governments."[6]

Dodge's claim can be supported by specific examples. As late as 1965, when Africans were designing a strategy to fight colonialism, it was widely reported that some missionaries were spying on them and joining the colonial army to fight against the people they claimed they were in Zimbabwe to serve.[7] The point to be noted is that the character of missionary Christianity was not entirely biblical Christianity. Instead, it was Western culture disguised as biblical principles. This kind of behavior made Africans believe that Western missionaries were preaching a gospel of Western superiority, not biblical Christianity. In the partnership between the colonialists and Christian missionaries, Africans saw little difference between the two, which cast suspicion on the motives of most missionaries.[8]

The third change has little to do with the focus of this book but assists readers in understanding the nature of the relationship between colonizers and missionaries. The primary purpose of the colonizers was to secure raw materials and to develop commerce for the benefit of both Europe and the white settlers. To achieve these two goals, colonizers needed a form of education that would prepare Africans to serve as cheap labor. Africans were to have a form of training through education quite different from the kind the Christian missionaries were persuading them to accept. This strategy created a quandary for missionaries and colonizers. It is important to note that while the colonial government believed that the educational policy of the missionaries was intended to "stabilize the faith of converts and assist in Christian character development,"[9] it was not designed to train them as laborers. Slowly the differences in educational policies pursued by the missionaries and the colonial government placed the two white institutions at a crossroads. Missionaries and colonizers had a symbiotic relationship. Each needed the other to survive in a foreign culture. This symbiotic relationship changed when missionaries realized that Africans needed education beyond practical training, a change signaled by the formation of the Southern Rhodesia Christian Conference in 190. Missionaries no longer espoused the same educational views as the 1956 colonizers. Rev. T. A. O'Farrell of the Methodist Church explained the importance of educating Africans beyond practical training: "The leaders whom we are developing today may become the pilots of their race in far larger areas than Rhodesia."[10]

The opening of mission schools, hospitals, colleges, and farms demonstrated the desires of Christian missionaries to pursue an educational policy beyond the rudiments for cheap labor, an education that would help Africans to read, interpret, and preach the Bible within their own contexts.[11] Difficult as it was to do, Christian missionaries eventually recognized that their acquiescence to colonial policy had cost them dearly, and they altered their course of action and began to educate Africans in terms that can be described as contextual. Although this was a hard road that took many years to travel and involved untold hardships, missionaries piloted the rise of a theological self-consciousness among Africans in a way colonizers failed to understand. Indeed, the colonizers would never fully understand many aspects of African traditional religious life.

With the fourth change, the use of the Bible as a textbook for classroom work in mission schools and as a sacred book in church led Africans to an awareness that their own destiny, in a world controlled by the whites, was in their own hands. I would venture to say that the translation of the English Bible into African dialects and languages greatly assisted indigenous people to discover not only Abraham but the entire historical, cultural, political, and social context of the Bible. I will return to this crucial hermeneutical factor later in this chapter, but it suffices to note that translation of the Bible into vernacular languages was the absolute key to a Pauline African theological formation. The opening of theological seminaries at the mission centers invigorated and rejuvenated a historical and theological consciousness that had lived in the hearts of Africans throughout history. The twentieth century saw this new consciousness rising so rapidly that it enabled Africans to recognize the arrogance of Europeans for what it was: a prescription that had to be eliminated if the religious, theological, and spiritual future of Africans was to be meaningful.

Some work on the role of missions has already been pursued by other African theologians; my concern in this book is to focus specifically on the effects of missionary encounters within the African religious cosmos, especially in the area of God, ancestry, culture, power, and identity. The self-consciousness of Africans was welcomed by Christian missionaries, who for the first time saw Africans as equals. One such missionary was Bishop Ralph Dodge, the first missionary bishop of Zimbabwe (1956–1964). Dodge had a profound commitment to sound, unsegregated education and theological education for blacks. He rejected racism in all its forms and insisted on handing over leadership to Africans. Similar messages were echoed by other educated black pastor-teachers like Aldon Mwamuka. In a message intended for his fellow Africans, Mwamuka said: "Let our behavior and our teaching be such that our pupils may go out of our schools as men and women who are ambassadors of the light and models of a good citizenship that members on the other side of the color line may have no excuse to deny us those things which, as members of the human family, are ours as well."[12] In order for this to happen, Mwamuka urged missionaries to provide Africans with an education that would help Africans raise questions about their place, role, and function in a global community. In 1946, the Methodist Church issued a statement calling for a change in their educational policy—one that would offer equality to students of all races.

It is noteworthy that the Shona people were quite aware of the presence of the Supreme Being, whom the missionaries referred to as God. Like the Greeks and Romans of Paul's day, Shona people believed in creation stories (though they came to accept the creation story as recorded in the book of Genesis). As the Bible was read in schools and churches, it was easy for Shona listeners to resonate with the biblical stories of creation as well as tales of wandering ancestors (Gen. 1:1-31; Deut. 26:4-5). Africans had known God, not with only one name but with many names, and this God was a genderless God. There were many similarities between African traditional religion and the Christian New Testament, especially when it came to a strong belief in the one Supreme Being of God. With regard to such knowledge, Andrew Lang makes the following observation: "We cannot but observe this reciprocal phenomenon: missionaries often find a native name and idea which answer so nearly to their conception of God that they adopt the idea and the name in teaching. Again on the other side, the savages, when first they hear the missionaries' account of God, recognize it, as do the Hurons and Bakwian, for what has always been familiar to them."[13] What we find in this observation is a religious notion that can be appropriated, cultivated, enlarged, and developed in concert with the God of Abraham, whom Africans appropriated and resonated with on the basis of spiritual ancestry. Recall that a vital element of Shona religion was the veneration of ancestors (Gen. 11:10-26). The concern for most Africans who came into contact with missionaries was how to transmute and transform African ways of worship that would align with Western models. The Bible was found to be a transformative vehicle for both ancestor veneration and worship of God. It is to this discovery that I now turn.

The Bible, Education, and Shona Culture

The Bible, the primary instrument used to influence Shona culture, did not completely wash out the indigenous modes of living, nor churn together new and old to form homogenous new identities. Rather, the encounter of synthesis and antithesis, of Shona traditional religion and the missionaries' Christian religion, fostered a new form of religion. A postcolonial term for this might be multiethnic Christianity: Christianity free from ethnocentrism or racism in that it embraces all nations, peoples, and races.[14] The Bible was presented as a colonial religious book, by white colonialists who assumed the role of "chosen people," a concept misappropriated by most colonialists who invaded south of the Sahara.[15] But the Bible was not the only item presented to Africans; the conquerors had a sword in the other hand.[16] What the Bible did was to remain in superimposition to the culture of the people, and its relationship to the African people was complex fashion. It was that complex relationship that gave birth to postcolonial Christianity. Christianity as a basis of new cultural relationships became during the colonial period a potent factor for controlling Africans in a new religious environment.

Colonial intentions were reinforced by the replacement of indigenous models of religion. Colonial readings negatively misrepresented the natives, and the exegetical strategies in commentaries and hermeneutical discourses greatly legitimized imperial control. In Zimbabwe, the Bible was used to designate Western culture as superior to all cultures, which resulted in the separation of the country's worship and educational institutions along racial lines. The suffering imposed on the Shona people by white minorities; the designation of less-than-full humanness; the justification of political, social, and economic oppression; and exploitation all had their origin in the way the Bible was used and in the interpretation of biblical texts.

Traditional African ancestors such as Mbuya Nehanda, Chaminuka, and Kaguvi were attacked by Christian missionaries, who regarded them as evil and not worthy to be part of a religious system of a people they sought to evangelize. African religious figures were replaced by figures from the Old and New Testaments, who were presented as people whose lives and faith-response to God provided lessons for those who came after. As a Christian minister and as an African New Testament theologian, I contend that what colonialists and missionaries overlooked was the cultural notion that all peoples and races have a record of models, known in cultural, political, and religious realms as founders and ancestors.[17] For Zimbabwean Shona people, such models were Nehanda, Chaminuka, Mkwati, Kaguvi, and other ethnic religious traditional leaders who opened new possibilities for all Shona people. Each nation has its own organized religious traditions led by its own venerated priests. Ancient Greeks, Romans, and Jews had their own venerated founders, and the Shona people tenaciously held onto their similar figures, whom they regarded as spiritual guardians of a nation.

Nehanda was a leading religious spirit medium in Zimbabwe, and her encounters with both missionaries and colonizers stand out as a record of hospitality, clash, and resistance. She fought relentlessly to defend her people's religious values against adulteration by Westerners, a cause for which she sacrificed her life when she was hanged by British colonialists in 1896.[18] Her last words, "My bones will rise again," were later immortalized in the hearts and minds of many young, gallant Zimbabwean fighters for African heritage and were celebrated on April 18, 1980, when Zimbabwe won its independence from the British. She died a martyr at the hands of British settlers on account of her own religious and cultural convictions. Nehanda was and still is remembered and venerated as the most influential and mystical of spiritual figures in the second war of liberation (1964–1979).

Nehanda should be a model for biblical and theological interpretation in Zimbabwe. I argue that Nehanda must be accorded an honored place alongside leading religious, cultural, and political leaders—such as Aeneas, who was celebrated as an ancestor of both Greeks and Romans, and Abraham, of the Jewish tradition and consequently of the Christian and Islamic faiths.[19] Each of these leaders played a reconciling role between peoples of different ethnic backgrounds, between Greeks and Romans, between Jews and Gentiles, and the continue to do so among nations of the twenty-first-century global world.[20]

While the Bible was used both as a textbook in classrooms and a sacred religious book in church, it also functioned as a religious and cultural resource for the Shona people. The Bible became useful for the formation and rebirth of multiethnic Shona faith and spirituality. Some explanation is needed for what may appear to be indiscriminate use of the Bible in the formation and reconstruction of multiethnic Shona Christianity. While many viewed the Bible as an ideological and powerful book, its reception by Africans marked a period of change in religious discourse. The change was brought about by a tension between the assumption on the part of Westerners that their knowledge gave them control over African culture, on the one hand, and the struggle of indigenous people to maintain their identity, on the other. In an attempt to appropriate the Western Bible, the Shona people engaged in a process of transformation.

Ideology is always a controversial word, referring possibly to the relation between indigenous cultures and social structures of power. This definition of ideology is in alignment with Edward Said's central theme of *Orientalism* as a body of knowledge that constructs the "Orient" as something the West can know and thereby control. Western knowledge stands in tension with the self-knowledge of the Orient.[21] Similarly, the Bible was seen to be a product of Western knowledge and power and, therefore, most people of African descent received it with suspicion. Dale Martin views ideology in terms of a linguistic, symbolic matrix that makes sense of and supports a particular exercise of power and the existing power structures. In postcolonial terms, this can be called the discourse of power.[22] However, ideology is more than ideas and religious beliefs; it evokes the dynamics of discourse and social power relations between the powerful and the less privileged cultures. In the case of Zimbabwe, ideology was seen in colonial and missionary rhetoric as an intentional way to denigrate indigenous people and, on the part of missionaries, as an attempt to evangelize. Ideology can be distinguished from propaganda, but both functioned simultaneously in the colonization and evangelization of Zimbabwe.

First, missionaries consciously used the Bible as an ideological book to persuade the indigenous people. Second, as a propaganda tool, the Bible represented power that was imposed from above by both missionaries and colonialists. In other words, Africans were simply to receive the book without question and learn to read it and use it in the church. What colonialists and missionaries overlooked or underestimated, however, was the power of education on human minds. On the rapidly changing frontier that was the colonial mission field of Zimbabwe, Shona people cautiously took note of the forms of power Westerners had access to, and then appropriated, adapted, and evolved them within their African-Christian worldview. The Bible ushered in a new period of what I call "African Enlightenment," placing confidence in African potential—a potential that sought to read the Bible according to indigenous hermeneutics. The influence of the Bible and Western religion slowly transformed the mind of Africans, and biblical reading opened new possibilities for both African culture and its religious systems.

In what ways did the Bible become a resource for Shona culture and religion? The question can be answered by saying, with Andrew Wallace-Hadrill, "Too often in cultural history, recourse is made to one of two metaphors: the metallurgical 'fusion' or the biological 'hybridity.'"[23] Indeed, what happened between Shona and Western cultures can rightly be labeled as "fusion *and* hybridization," in which a blending and a cross-fertilization process allowed Africans to retain their past as a source of identity and to appropriate both Old and New Testament biblical models of identity rooted in ancestry. In this regard, the Bible functioned first as an educational textbook in the classroom for religious and moral education. Missionaries employed religious and moral education to cover such areas as evangelism; training in worship, prayer, and Christian character; instruction in the Bible and Christian doctrine;

and the Christian interpretation of the meaning and purpose of life.[24] The concern was not to develop the Africans' skills; rather, the goal as perceived by missionaries was to develop natives who had balance, self-control, higher standards of values, and a new moral sense for life in the community. The objective was to simply teach the African to read and interpret Scripture. Rev. A. L. Buckwalter, a missionary at Mutambara mission in the eastern part of Zimbabwe, reported at a conference that an exceptionally good girl at the school was able to read the whole New Testament in her native language.[25] The impetus was not to impart knowledge for itself, but to train people who would go out into the villages to share not only academic knowledge but also the saving knowledge of God through Jesus Christ.

While this form of education helped missionaries, it was also a danger in that both teachers and students were religiously and spiritually awakened with information gained from reading the Bible. Indigenous readers of the Bible were able to raise questions with biblical texts, as well as adding their own voices to the interpretations of other faith communities. Students memorized facts or portions of Scripture that resonated with the African ways of religious and cultural living. Knowing the names of the twelve tribes of Israel or giving the list of the kings of Judah or the places Paul visited was probably the beginning of indigenous religious incubation. Similarly, educated Shona were able to answer all the questions of baptism without being Christians. As new converts, Shona people were able to read the Bible not only in English but also in vernacular language. Thus the Bible began to slip from the hands of the missionaries into the hearts, minds, and souls of indigenous people.

The ability to read and interpret biblical text using indigenous or theological vernacular hermeneutics meant that the Shona people had the capacity to own the Bible as theirs and to interrogate Scripture in ways consonant with African worldviews. However, as their religious education progressed, African minds began to grow in their insights, and they developed right attitudes about people such as Abraham, and how God was manifested in their own lives, and how their lives were transformed. In this process, personal experiences of God among Africans stirred their spiritual imaginations and moved them to act in ways that overturned colonial missionary assumptions. The Bible allowed Africans to be conscious of their own identity, their own history, and their own traditions in the midst of colonial and missionary encounters. So while missionaries perceived education as a way to communicate the gospel to African people, that view was in some tension with the "cultural" mission of Victorian colonialism.

As a student in colonial education and later an educator in postcolonial Zimbabwe, I vividly remember how, in the first session of class, known as MRE, an abbreviation for "moral and religious education," an outstanding part of this session was marked by the song in the epigraph of this chapter. Standing outside early in the morning, one would hear the words: "Father Abraham had many sons / Many sons had Father Abraham / I am one of them and so are you / so let's all praise the Lord!" From 1890 to 1980, this song shaped and molded every facet of education in Zimbabwe. Pastor-teachers in every school functioned both as colonial educators and preachers of the word of God.[26]

Missionary education was basically the ability to read the Bible in the vernacular and in English and the ability to teach the Bible to other local people. An exceptionally good student was expected to be able to read the New Testament in Shona. The nature and mode of education for Africans became a subject of intense debate among colonial officials and missionaries. The questions at the center of this debate were: What kind of education should the Africans receive? What is the intended goal of this education? Answers to these questions created conflict because, on the one hand, missionaries wanted African education to include literacy and religious instruction. On the other hand, colonial officials wanted only education that would produce cheap and obedient laborers instead of critical thinkers. Colonialists promoted a form of education that would allow Africans to be the hewers of wood and the drawers of water for their masters.

Two observations must be made at this point regarding the philosophical and theological educational objectives in African education. The first is that the Christian missionaries readily recognized that if the views of the colonial officials about the character of education for Africans prevailed, the resulting educational process would reduce their own influence in the lives of the people, whom they believed could only change for the good. The missionaries' recognition of the differing goals of education was a painful experience that caused them to wonder if they had lost the major objective of stabilizing the faith of converts. It troubled the missionaries that the nature of colonial education relative to Africans would require the surrender of educational policies to government officials, and religious values would be rendered meaningless with the emergence of a totally secular education.

The second observation is that the missionaries realized that to regard African traditional religion as meaningless and primitive and to expect the Africans to discard the customs of their ancestors during a period when their land had been invaded was to expect them to deny and discard their cultural identity and religious practices. This negative attitude by white settlers toward cultural essentials of African identity did not help missionary objectives. With the policies of colonial education in place, missionaries became alienated from Africans, thus losing the influence they should have exerted. Later, missionaries became aware that their influence had been damaged and began to critically question the policies of colonial education. The loss of influence is expressed by Geoffrey Kapenzi, a Zimbabwean theologian, who explains how the thinking among missionaries was detrimental to their cause and how they were losing the struggle for control of the education of Africans: "The vast majority of missionaries referred to the Africans as the descendants of Ham and as Kaffir Natives. Therefore, the missionaries did not practice Biblical Christianity, but colonial religion in which African-missionary relations were set in their colonial pattern of masters and servants, superiors and inferiors."[27]

It is clear from this observation that Western missionaries from the beginning had one major objective—to convert Shona people to Christianity. There was nothing wrong with this objective in itself. That was how the Romans had promoted their culture. But what was questionable about the work of missionaries in the nineteenth century was that they equated Christianity with Western culture. They seemed to confuse the teaching of biblical Christianity with the practices of Western culture. As imperialists and colonizers, they regarded themselves as vanguards of Christian faith and elevated themselves as promoters of civilization. The former cause of Christianizing the Africans was tainted with a cultural ego manifested in most Victorian missionaries. However, they believed that before the educational process could begin, the Africans must show their willingness to accept Christianity.

In failing to appreciate the positive attributes of African culture, colonialists and missionaries made it hard for the two cultures to create the environment of understanding that biblical Christianity promoted. With the exception of Ralph Dodge, the first American missionary Bishop of Zimbabwe, other Western missionaries like Robert Moffat and David Livingstone never fully understood the Shona religious worldview. Difficult as it was to do, Western missionaries eventually recognized that their acquiescence to colonial education had cost them dearly and a change was needed. From 1936 until the end of colonization, in 1980, another form of missionary activity emerged, this time not from Victorian missionaries but from an American perspective. To this I now turn.

Mission Centers as Incubators of Postcolonial Shona Christian Readings of the Bible

While church history in Zimbabwe is fraught with analytical theological opportunities for Bible exegetes and commentators, it is important to establish the poignant fact that mission centers, whether Protestant or Catholic, were indeed incubators of what is now called postcolonial African Christianity. This form of Christianity is multiethnic in character because it embraces all the diverse ethnicities and races in Zimbabwe. I would like to challenge the assumptions of most Western biblical scholars who view postcolonialism as a time that marked the formal ending of the empire. Postcolonialism does not signify the end of the empire; rather, it refers to a reactive or dissident reading of the Bible undertaken by people both during and after colonization.[28] It is probably fitting to say that postcolonialism was birthed during the colonial period and is called *postcolonial Christianity* in this book. Postcolonialism should be viewed as a discourse that engages simultaneously with and against the claims of empire representatives. John Wesley Z. Kurewa, a Zimbabwean theologian and former vice chancellor of Africa University, observes that "education, as perceived by the early missionaries, was basically a way of communicating the gospel to the African people and was not an end itself."[29] The poignancy of this observation was manifested in the establishment of mission centers. These centers took different forms, such as Roman Catholic, British Methodist, United Methodist Episcopal/United Methodist, Anglican, Lutheran, Baptist, and the United Congregational Church of Southern Africa.[30] Common to all these mission centers was a certain reading and interpretation of both the Old and New Testaments of the Bible.[31]

Each mission center had an elementary and high school, teacher training college, and sports center, as well as a hospital where local people were exposed to Western forms of living. In other words, mission centers were functionally similar to the gymnasium during the penetration of Greek education and culture in Palestinian Judaism.[32] Mission centers were in many ways major centers of literacy for Africans. In their endeavor to spread the gospel, missionary groups made it clear to colonizers that education was a mission priority in the liberation of people. The colonial government wanted Africans to train as cheap laborers. Although it is hard to fix a specific date, 1936 seems to signal a change of position by missionaries. The formation of the Southern Rhodesia Christian Conference in 1906 demonstrated that the missionaries and colonial establishment no longer espoused the same view regarding the education of the Shona people.

For the first time, missionaries made it clear to the colonial government that the leaders they were developing and educating would become the pilots of their indigenous people in far larger areas than simply Zimbabwe. Thus missionaries viewed theological and secular education as complementary programs. I stress the fact that for missionaries, education was primarily a tool to communicate the gospel to the Shona people, and mission centers were significant for four reasons: first, they offered a space for Shona people to read the Bible in their own language; second, in that space, the Shona people could for the first time interpret the Bible for themselves; third, the mission centers provided an opportunity for Africans to develop their own hymnody; and, fourth, they brought about the rise of a contextualized African Christianity. I will now examine each of these in turn.

First, mission centers offered a public space for Shona people to read and analyze the Bible using vernacular language. Both preachers and laypeople were supposed to be familiar with the whole Bible, from Genesis to Revelation. Theologically, mission centers had one objective: to train and teach the African to read and interpret the Bible in both English and Shona.[33] Life-situation approaches took center stage as missionaries became familiar with the world of Africans, especially in the area of sickness, barrenness, hunger, and poverty. The methods through which the Bible was taught in mission centers took the form of drama, catechism, music, and the memorization of Bible verses. Along with this was the profession of faith, which in the African church meant an invitation from the pastor to the laypeople to accept the word of God (Isa. 55:10–11). The translation of the Bible into various ethnic Zimbabwe languages assisted indigenous people in noticing affinities between Christian New Testament stories and African mythologies, especially stories of Abraham as a wandering ancestor.

Shona Bible readers were exposed to the idea that there were other worlds besides theirs and that the Bible carries other mythologies of human foundations. Genealogical stories of Abraham became points of attraction for Shona readers. The pride of the Jews in the precedence of their ancestors, especially Abraham, Sarah, Isaac, and Jacob, held great appeal for Africans in mission schools. The stories of Abraham and his achievements in Gen. 12–22 exercised unbroken fascination among Shona theologians and Bible readers. Few Shona people could resist the incidents of circumcision, wandering, childlessness, faith, and eventually becoming the father of many nations. The Genesis narrative of Abraham and God portrays a complex story of struggle and virtue, especially on the part of an ancestor who would end up establishing a new community. It was through missionary education that Africans discovered

Abraham to be a primordial and foundational figure. Abraham, like any African ancestor, appealed to Shona Christians not only as an archetype of faith response to God's call and promises but also as an embodiment of paradigmatic values. The paradigmatic value applies also to the question of cultures.

The biblical accounts concerning Abraham illustrate Israel's standpoint in regard to its surrounding peoples. Abraham is a representative of a Gentile, coming from pagan nations, although he severs his link with the Shona people to become the starting point of a new history. Similarly, the Shona ancestors were people who embarked on journeys in search of better pastures for their cattle and more productive land for their peoples. Abraham's journeys resonated well with the Shona people, whose reading of Gen. 11:27—12:9, especially 12:1-3, pointed to the life of an itinerant. Thus, for Shona people, faith takes the form of a journey; Gen. 12:1-3 introduces the metaphor of journey as a way of characterizing the life of faith. This will be the subject of chapter 3, but it suffices to note that the life of faith/wandering keeps Israel in pursuit of the promised land, an idea that led to the birth of political nationalism in Zimbabwe.

Second, mission centers offered a public space for Shona Christians to scrutinize the Bible openly. As people who were outside of the West's age of reason and the Enlightenment, local readers inspected and found ways of contextualizing Old and New Testament claims. Shona people who resided in mission schools and attended church services and Sunday school classes took it upon themselves to make their own readings of the very book that was so often used against them. Mission centers played the role of decentering the message both of the Bible and of those who claimed to know it better. In other words, the a priori claims for the purity and wholesomeness of Christianity and the intellectual presuppositions of both Europeans and Americans were combatively encountered for the first time. In the mission schools, the program of contextualization that gave birth to multiethnic Christianity was established. The program of biblical contextualization must be understood as life-situation readings of biblical texts. African readers discovered some similarities between their culture and that of the Old Testament. The Old Testament refers to God as "God of the patriarchs," and among Shona cultures, God is equally referred to as "God of the ancestors."[34] This discovery led to the appropriation of Abraham as one who integrates nations, thus making him the connecting link to all nations.

Third, mission centers provided an opportunity for Shona readers to assert the virtues of African faiths and songs. There were at least two revelatory postcolonial moments during the height of mission establishment that have a deep significance for Shona Christianity. One was the development of the printing press at Hartzell Mission School in Mutare, east of Harare, and the translation of the English Bible into local languages. Added to these printed translations was the development of the hymnody of the mission churches among various ethnic peoples of Zimbabwe. Thus, from 1890 to 1950, hymns in Shona, Ndẹbele, and related dialects were circulating in and around mission schools.[35] The training of local theologians and preachers meant a shift of responsibilities, especially in the proclamation of the Old and New Testament. Until 1900, it was Western missionaries and Western Bible scholars who had the resources and power to educate, preach, and train the indigenous teachers and theologians on the interpretation of the Bible. But now the responsibility was given to local pastor-teachers, who were now gospel ambassadors to their own people. Missionaries were quick to realize that locally trained people could be entrusted with the task of preaching the gospel to rural people. A successfully educated African evangelist was supposed to read the entire Old and New Testaments and interpret their message using the language of the laypeople. This third perspective leads to the fourth—and perhaps more crucial—role of missionary education, which is the Africanization/contextualization of the gospel.

Fourth, mission centers provided a forum that piloted the rise of religious consciousness among Africans in a way that missionaries failed to understand. Indeed, they never fully understood many aspects of Shona religiosity, spirituality, piety, morality, and ethics. The force of this consciousness was well expressed by Bishop Ralph E. Dodge of the American Methodist Church of Southern Rhodesia and Nyasaland. Speaking at a conference in 1938, Bishop Dodge argued and warned, "There is room for white and black to live side by side. Neither is independent of the other. The white man's place in Africa depends on a modus vivendi based on justice and granting the Native people opportunities for development."[36]

The impact of these words was felt by many leading missionaries, who felt that theological conditions were shifting and that it was time for missionaries to recognize the rights of Africans as equal partners in the interpretation of biblical texts. The adaptation of African understanding and interpretation of the Christian faith that affirms the living realities of the African context is the Africanization of faith.[37] As African preachers took the gospel to surrounding rural areas, the church began to expand and more people were attracted to the gospel of Jesus Christ. There was indeed a thirst for the supernatural among Shona Christian converts. The translation of the Bible into Shona languages helped white missionaries to see some errors in some of the theological injections of Western religions. An illustration of this error is seen in the version of Shona theology where the Supreme Being or God of the Shona people has no gender specificity, yet in Western Christianity there is a tension. African pastor-teachers were able to contextualize the message of the Bible and make it relevant to local people.

In the course of their theological and secular education, African theologians found connecting centers and figures, and one such figure was the apostle Paul. Preaching on biblical characters was one of the favorite approaches to biblical preaching in Zimbabwe. It is no wonder that people have said that African preachers use the Old Testament more than the New Testament because preachers love to preach about Old Testament figures like Abraham, Sarah, Jacob, and Moses, as well as Paul of the New Testament. In Africa, Christian believers in both mission and rural churches were quick to identify with such biblical characters. These characters resonated well with people's ancestors. In the case of the Shona people, they were able to appropriate and contextualize these figures as ancestors of faith.[38] The central point lifted from each character was the gospel, that is, the saving acts of God that surrounded each of the figures.

As one who has been involved in the life of the church in Zimbabwe for many years and has been educated in African and North American contexts, and now teaches New Testament studies in an American seminary, I argue that Africans discovered Paul to be a theological and religious partner in three major ways. First, Paul's Jewish background was an essential element in the religious and cultural awakening of African culture. Second, Paul's religious-cultural autobiography in Gal. 1:11–24 had great appeal to most Africans, who were zealous for their own cultural ideals. The third and most crucial element was Paul's claim as an apostle to the Gentiles—a claim he creatively enunciated and systematized. Paul starts with his Jewish religious heritage. He does so in relation to what lies at hand, namely, the Torah—an embodiment of the Jewish heritage, one he firmly believed to be the text of the God of all peoples, nations, and races, one who created heaven and earth, and therefore the entire human family. Paul came to be in radical tension with his own cultural heritage, not because it was unsound but because his call to be an apostle to the Gentiles had cast a shadow over any claims for cultural superiority or absolutism, whether Jewish or other.[39]

The third and most revolutionary element has to do with Paul's creative construction of Abraham as a spiritual ancestor of "all who share the faith of Abraham, for he is the father of all of us" (Rom. 4:16–17). Paul's critical stance toward his own culture allowed Africans to engage critically with their own

African traditional religion. They did so in ways that even missionaries failed to understand because ancestry was a foreign concept to Western culture. For now, it suffices to say that both Paul's culture and gospel resonated deeply with the culture and gospel of Africans. I would suggest, therefore (with a certain degree of trepidation), that Africans discovered Paul to be a cross-cultural apostle who was opposed to the claims of Western imperialism. Through the eyes of the African church, Paul was a model championing the seriousness of God's irrevocable design to draw all people to the divine. Thus the death and resurrection of Jesus had inaugurated the new age in which Paul, like Peter, discovered on a Gentile frontier that "God is no respecter of persons but that in every nation anyone who fears him and does what is acceptable to him" (Acts 10:34-35).

Indeed, the discovery and appropriation of Pauline Christianity and the spiritual construction of Abraham gave birth to Shona multiethnic Christianity. Clearly the idea of Gentiles as also coming within the full inner circle of salvation resonated with Africans, assisting them to appropriate the apostle Paul as a cross-cultural missionary, a Jew who sought to be "all things to all people" in order to win others to the gospel of Jesus Christ (1 Cor. 9:19-23). Theologically and sociologically, Paul helped Africans recognize that humanity does not live in isolation, but the community is a dimension of human existence—an existence that crosses genealogical boundaries.

The genius of the African discovery of Paul and Abraham as theological and spiritual dialogue partners allowed the guardians of African culture and religion—namely, the chiefs—to welcome missionaries, and even give them permission to build schools, hospitals, churches, and training centers. Reading and singing stories of Abraham in the Old Testament were no longer perceived as mere educational moments but were times of engagement with and against the ideologies of the empire. The significance and function of the "Father Abraham Song" among indigenous people in Zimbabwe marked an era of reformation, religious awakening, evolution, and challenge.

Indeed, it was a resource of religious awakening and reformation because the song enlightened people to the reconciling effect of Abraham, not only as founder of biblical faith, but also as a figure whom Africans could appropriate into their ancestral cosmology and, consequently, assist African believers in accepting and contextualizing Jesus Christ into the category of spiritual and faith ancestry. The genius of Shona Christianity, born during the encounter with colonialism and missionizing, is its concern for all the peoples to be brothers and sisters. Having read and interpreted Paul and Abraham, Shona Christians devised ways of worship that were applicable to their context, culture, and values. In the next chapter, I will make the perhaps surprising claim that neither British nor European missionaries talked about Paul or Abraham. My claim is that Africans discovered these figures through exposure to the Bible as a classroom textbook and as book to be read in church on Sunday morning and in a catechism class. What was born from this exposure was a form of Christianity—a postcolonial Christianity—whose basis, paradoxically, is the truth claim made by the missionaries, but in a way they did not anticipate: Christian discourse hinges on one thing—faith in Jesus Christ.

Notes

1. Canaan Sodindo Banana, *The Church and the Struggle for Zimbabwe: From the Programme to Combat Racism to Combat Theology* (Gweru, Zimbabwe: Mambo Press, 1996), 19.

2. Education for the Shona people was a contested issue between colonizers and missionaries. Colonial masters advocated for an education that would produce cheap laborers. Missionaries wanted education that included literacy and religious instruction for purposes of evangelism in vernacular languages.

3. John Wesley Z. Kurewa, *The Church in Mission: A Short History of the United Methodist Church in Zimbabwe, 1897–1997* (Nashville: Abingdon, 1997), 29.

4. Ibid.

5. I will use the phrase *Victorian colonizers* in this book to refer to "missionaries" whose aim was to colonize, conquer, and occupy Zimbabwe. These "missionaries" include such figures as David Livingstone, Cecil John Rhodes, and Henry Morton Stanley, who came with the supremacy of colonial commercial enterprise.

6. Ralph Dodge, "The African Church Now and in the Future" (unpublished essay, 1966). On file at the Old Mutare Mission Church Library, Zimbabwe.

7. See D. E. Needham, E. K. Mashingaidze, and N. Bhebhe, eds., *From Iron Age to Independence: A History of Central Africa* (Harare, Zimbabwe: Longman, 1984), 96.

8. See Canaan Sodindo Banana, *The Church and the Struggle for Zimbabwe: From the Programme to Combat Racism to Combat Theology* (Gweru, Zimbabwe: Mambo Press, 1996), 110–35. Here Banana documents the responses of African religious and missionary leaders to Ian Smith's Unilateral Declaration of Independence, a declaration whose agenda was to deny Africans their religious cultural heritage.

9. Harold Jowitt, "The Annual Report of the Director of Native Education" (1928), 15, found at the University of Zimbabwe Library.

10. T. A. O'Farrell, "Report to Annual Conference," *Official Journal of the Methodist Church* (1928): 30, found in the United Methodist Archive at Old Mutare Mission in Zimbabwe.

11. See Dickson A. Mungazi, *The Honored Crusade: Ralph Dodge's Theology of Liberation and Initiative for Social Change in Zimbabwe* (Gweru, Zimbabwe: Mambo Press, 1991), 25–29.

12. Aldon Mwamuka, in a presidential address during an annual conference of the African Teachers Association, Mutare, July 31, 1945. In the Zimbabwean National Archives.

13. Andrew Lang, *Making Religion* (New York: Longman, Green, 1889), 229.

14. See Daniel Boyarin, *A Radical Jew: Paul and the Politics of Identity* (Berkeley: University of California Press, 1994), 228–42.

15. See Canaan Banana, "The Case for a New Bible," in *Voices from the Margin: Interpreting the Bible in Third World*, ed. R. S. Surgirtharajah (Maryknoll, NY: Orbis, 2000), 73.

16. See *Missionary Review of the World* 17, no. 12 (1894): 882.

17. For a detailed discussion on the centrality of ancestral traditions, see Andrew Wallace-Hadrill, "Knowing the Ancestors," in *Rome's Cultural Revolution*, ed. Andrew Wallace-Hadrill (Cambridge: Cambridge University Press, 2008), 213–58.

18. Needham, Mashingaidze, and Bhebe, eds., *From Iron Age to Independence*, 129. See also David Martin and Phyllis Johnson, *The Struggle for Zimbabwe: The Chimurenga War* (New York: Monthly Review Press, 1981), 78.

19. Aeneas is the Greco-Roman hero who journeyed from Troy to found the line of the Romans. Abraham is the father of the Israelites through his son Isaac, whose mother was Sarah (Gen. 7:1-19). In Islamic tradition, Abraham is considered a prophet of Islam, the ancestor of Muhammad, through Abraham's son Ishmael, whose mother was Hagar. See Brannon M. Wheeler, *Prophets in the Quran: An Introduction to the Quran and Muslim Exegesis* (London: Continuum, 2002), 106–7.

20. Arnold Momigliano, *On Pagans, Jews, and Christians* (Middletown, CT: Wesleyan University Press, 1987), 264–84. In this book, Momigliano documents a cultural story of the reconciliation of Greeks and Romans, a story of ancestral construction similar to the one Paul creatively constructs in the Epistle to the Romans, esp. Rom. 4:1-25.

21. Edward Said, *Orientalism* (New York: Vintage, 1978), 195. Some reference works in the United States describe the word *Oriental* as pejorative; Merriam-Webster's *New Collegiate Dictionary*, 11th ed., for instance, mentions that it is "sometimes offensive." In this book, I use it simply to refer to Eurasia, Asia, and Africa

22. Dale B. Martin, *The Corinthian Body* (New Heaven: Yale University Press, 1995), 8.

23. Andrew Wallace-Hadrill, *Rome's Cultural Revolution* (Cambridge: Cambridge University Press, 2008), 7.

24. See Geoffrey Z. Kapenzi, *The Clash of Cultures: Christian Missionaries and the Shona of Rhodesia* (Washington, DC: University Press of America, 1978), 72.

25. See Kurewa, *Church in Mission*, 47.

26. Pastor-teachers were trained African missionaries who were sent into the remote parts of Zimbabwe to teach and establish churches.

27. Kapenzi, *Clash of Cultures*, 21.

28. See Banana, "Case for a New Bible," 17–32.

29. Kurewa, *Church in Mission*, 47.

30. The word *mission* is used in this book to refer to two facets: (1) the mission to control and tame Africans by invading their land and taming them into hewers of wood and drawers of water and (2) mission as a theological endeavor of liberating Africans from heathenism.

31. Banana, *The Church and the Struggle for Zimbabwe*, 35–55.

32. The fusion and diffusion of Hellenistic culture and education into Palestinian Judaism is well developed in Martin Hengel, *Judaism and Hellenism: Studies in the Encounter during the Early Hellenistic Period* (Eugene, OR: Wipf & Stock, 2003), 58–91.

33. See Kurewa, *Church in Mission*, 46.

34. For a detailed discussion on cultural readings and contextualization of the Bible in Africa, see John Wesley Z. Kurewa, *Preaching and Cultural Identity: Proclaiming the Gospel in Africa* (Nashville: Abingdon, 2000), 15–31.

35. See M. F. C. Bourdillon, SJ, ed., *Christianity South of the Zambezi* (Harare, Zimbabwe: Mambo Press, 1977), 2:103–20.

36. Ralph E. Dodge, "American Methodist Conference in Zambia," 3 (1938). Most of the documents of missionary work in Africa are housed at Old Mutare Mission in Zimbabwe.

37. Kurewa, *Church in Mission*, 172–73

38. See especially Deut. 26:4-5; Rom. 4:1-25; and Heb. 11:4-39.

39. See Boyarin, *A Radical Jew*, 39–56. Boyarin presents a panoramic discussion of how Paul wrestled with his own culture, especially the claims of the Torah.

3

Postcolonial Shona Christianity

What then shall we say about Abraham,
our ancestor according to the flesh?

–ROMANS 4:1

THE DISCOURSE OF PAULINE CHRISTIANITY

The subject of ancestry and descent from a powerful ancestor or founder holds a central place in politics, religion, and social life.[1] The Romans and Greeks of the Augustan era (fourth century BCE) claimed a powerful pedigree from Aeneas.[2] The apostle Paul, who represented the religious-social world of Palestine, claimed descent from Abraham (Gal. 1:13-16). While the Shona people have tribal ancestors, the period between 1890 and 1980 saw an amalgamation of tribes and ethnic groups into one distinctive nation who for the first time claimed Mbuya Nehanda as the ancestress of all Shona people.[3] Nehanda had a great deal of religious and political influence in many regions of Zimbabwe, as did Aeneas and Abraham in their regions of the world. The histories of these ancient nations demonstrate to modern-day readers the mythological underpinnings of all peoples, races, and nations.[4]

People have stories to tell about their gods, their male and female ancestors, and the achievements of their cities and villages. Ancestors, or *maiores*, are held as models of virtue and wisdom, whose distinctive identity the present generation is to emulate. To invoke an ancestor is to invoke a stable model of legitimacy: and indeed, ancestors are most invoked when legitimacy is most at stake. Ancestors are also invoked for purposes of a coordinate, measuring time in generations. Thus the acceptance of Nehanda resonated well with the African conception of what constituted an African. With the British flag flying in the heart of Harare, which the colonial government renamed Fort Salisbury, in honor of the imperialist British prime minister, the name of the spiritual ancestress Nehanda needed to be invoked. Invoking and naming ancestors was one of the cardinal virtues about Greco-Roman history; and failure to do so meant betrayal of tradition, culture, and religion. Therefore, invoking Nehanda during and after the colonial period is analogous to the Roman tradition—a tradition that Paul utilized to reconstruct Abraham in a worldview that upheld allegiance, loyalty, and value to founding ancestors.[5]

Paul's reconstruction of Abraham is beyond politics, religion, and social concerns; he presents Abraham as the "spiritual and faith ancestor" of all nations who would believe in the death and resurrection of Jesus Christ (Rom. 3:21-26). Few theologians have yet discovered the importance of biblical genealogies for twenty-first-century Christian believers. Two of the gospels, Matthew and Luke, provide long genealogies of Jesus Christ. The Pauline notion of Jesus Christ as the Son of God and the language of Abrahamic ancestry resonated deeply with Shona spirituality and led to a contextualization of Paul's gospel and theology within African Christianity.[6]

Throughout this book, I claim that we, the Shona people, during the colonial missionary period, felt a strong affinity for Paul's idea of ancestry, and we creatively appropriated selected aspects of Euro-American Christianity into our African Christianity. At the same time, Euro-American missionaries introduced a Paul who was largely Western in orientation. Their reading and interpretation of Paul was shaped by a Western view of individualism and exclusivism. But the Paul whom Africans read in the vernacular Bible was a cross-cultural apostle who claimed to have become "all things to all people" in order to win them to the gospel (1 Cor. 9:19-23).

Africans also resonated with Paul because his gospel was about the "impartial righteousness of God," whereby cultural superiority was confronted with the power of God's grace (Rom. 1:18—4:25).[7] This Shona reading of Paul can be labeled as identification by association: one in which their condition of being colonized stirred the consciousness of Shona religious leaders, driving them to a transformed plane of religious-cultural awareness, awakening, and renewal. Paul did the same thing in his Greco-Roman context, a view that Western New Testament scholarship has not yet discovered possibly because the concept of ancestry is associated with colonial domination. Or could it be that Western culture is focused more on individualism and individual rights?

The Western worldview emphasizes the nuclear family, whereas postcolonial Christians place great emphasis on the common bond of all human beings. But could it also be that colonially oriented cultures have difficulty understanding Paul because of not wanting to acknowledge the spirituality of

Abraham? Postcolonialism argues that Western colonizing nations have secret ancestors of whom they are proud and who define their identities. For the British it was Cecil John Rhodes, and for the Greeks and Romans it was Aeneas. For the Jewish people it was "Abraham according to the flesh" (Rom. 4:1). Paul's appeal to Abraham is a response to the *Aeneid*—the dominant ancestry, the imperial ancestry of Paul's day—and the apostle opposed it with a creative reconstruction of Abraham. My discovery of the Aeneas-Abraham connection is new, but it fits the experiences of Shona Christianity.

The comparison between Aeneas and Abraham is especially powerful for African Christians because Paul did what the Shona people did. He did not just walk onto the scene already knowing about and imposing his ancestry, but he actively and selectively appropriated aspects of the *Aeneid* story and made it theologically central to his Jesus story. While this will be dealt with in chapter 4, it suffices to say that the usefulness of this comparison opens new possibilities into the exegesis of Paul, especially in the context of African Christianity.

Romans 3:21—4:25 in the Context of Colonial and Postcolonial African Christianity

The affinities between Paul and Shona Christians lie not only in the use of ancestral language but also in the way the apostle articulates the meaning and nature of God. The God of the precolonial Shona people was intricately involved with ancestors and was manifested through ancestral figures. Yet missionaries completely overlooked or ignored a worldview that included ancestors. They preached and taught Paul in propositional terms: an apostle without regard for ancestors. The diatribe of Rom. 3:27-31 is absolutely the key passage to the understanding of Paul's resonance with the Shona people. When Christian missionaries attempted to preach about God, they often missed the religious cultural heart of their listeners. First, they spoke of God without taking into account the fact that for the Shona people, God was a Supreme Being who was not individualistic but communal in nature. Second, before the missionaries came to Africa, practitioners of African traditional religion had a strong belief in the Supreme Being, or *Mwari*.[8] In time, Shona Christians, through their vernacular interpretations not only of Paul but also of the Genesis and Exod. 3:15-16,began to articulate this resonance with Pauline theology.

The exposure to moral and religious education offered Africans an opportunity to read and eulogize the ancestry of Abraham in ways foreign to missionaries.[9] For Westerners, their God was individually oriented, yet the God whom the Shona read in Paul's letter in Rom. 3:27-31 was an inclusive

God of Jews and Gentiles—and, consequently, of the Shona people.[10] In Shona religious cosmology, the Supreme Being is the inexhaustible source of life and vital power and the unique agent of the vital breath of life, whose manifestation is recognized through nature and speaks to all people through ancestors. This religious cosmology is clearly formulated especially in Exod. 3:15–16, where God implicitly reveals himself to Moses: "Say to the people of Israel, Yahweh, the God of your ancestor, the God of Abraham, the God of Isaac, and the God of Jacob, has sent me to you: This is my name forever, and thus I am to be remembered throughout all generations. Go and gather the elders of Israel together, and say to them, Yahweh, the God of your ancestors, the God of Abraham, of Isaac and of Jacob, has appeared to me." This is the same God whom Africans learned from Paul, a God who encompasses all peoples and nations by offering salvation to *all* on the basis of grace alone.[11] In colonial context, καύχησις ("boasting") was exhibited by missionaries who assumed they possessed a correct reading of Paul. In African thought, boasting indicated a form of pride that was against the theological notion of the essence of being human. The Paul whom the Shona people read in Romans appeared to be an apostle who advocated for equality in the midst of cultural diversity. For Paul, honor granted through grace alone eliminates the basis of all human boasting, the result of which is the humiliation of colonial arrogance.[12]

Another theological aspect that captured the religious imagination of the Shona people was Paul's notion of the righteousness of God (Rom. 3:21). Paul believed that something decisive had happened in the events surrounding Jesus of Nazareth. This sense of a decisive event in his own present life is signaled by the phrase "But now" in 3:21. The idea is also repeated in verse 26, "in the now times." Paul describes what had happened in verse 21, "Now the righteousness of God has been revealed." The revelation is qualified by two phrases: "apart from the law" and "through faith." It is this "righteousness of God," through faith in Jesus Christ, justifying both the Shona and colonizers without distinction, that appealed to African-Christian converts.

One of the strongest connections between Paul's Jesus and African ancestors is the belief in the blood of Jesus Christ as expiation for all peoples, races, and nations. The incarnation of Jesus resonated well with Zimbabwe's belief in the "living dead," who continue to unite a vast web of kinship ties. The New Testament provides the kinship relationship that defines Jesus as a human being fully present within the community of faith. Romans 8:29 refers to Jesus as "the firstborn within a large family," of which African Christians are part. Theologically, Jesus Christ, who founded lineages, sealed the faith of Abraham, who embodied the essence of the gospel.[13] The second aspect of Paul that resonated with the Shona was on the God who revealed himself through Jesus Christ, a concept that is authentically African.[14] Against this background, the focal position of faith in Jesus becomes understandable among Shona Christians. In this regard, Africans learned something new about the role and function of Jesus. They began to understand Jesus in four main theological categories: Jesus as the Son of God; Jesus as a "Black Messiah" who is also proclaimed as *Christus Victor*; Jesus as the one crucified who takes our sins on himself; and Jesus as the one to come who will bring God's kingdom in its fullness.

First, they appropriated Jesus as the Son of God, one who embodies the very nature of God. Instead of simply accepting him as Jesus, Shona Christian leaders and biblical theologians began to use the term "Black Messiah," one who stands at the gates of heaven playing the role of the mediator between God and humanity.[15] Christologically, Jesus gained a new place among Shona Christians, who appropriated him as one who will admit only his own followers into the kingdom of God. Thus Shona Christians believed Paul's idea of God who acquits people of their sins through faith in Jesus Christ (Rom. 1:16–17) to be the key to salvation. Just as the ancestor had traditionally acted as mediator between people and God, so the Black Christ became the mediator effecting the salvation of his people. One of the most powerful reasons for this development among Shona Christians was humanity's longing for a concrete revelation here and now, the visible God who will be approached by people. The result of this newfound role of Jesus was that it led to an appropriation of his role at a higher level than that of tribal ancestor. Jesus met the need for a greater vital force among both Christian individuals and communities.[16]

Second, Jesus as a Black Messiah was proclaimed in all villages as the *Christus Victor*, the one who triumphs over all evil powers and forces (Col. 2:15). The Shona people proclaimed that the missionaries' gospel was incomplete because it suppressed both the biblical conception of Christ as the image of God and the message of the Holy Spirit. These two aspects gained a renewed understanding among African Christians, whose belief in spirit possession was ingrained in their religious and cultural worldview. Here again we see that Paul became a theological catalyst and partner in the explicit recognition of the kingship of Christ. This acknowledgement is especially powerful because Paul did what Shona Christians finally came to grips with—he contextualized the message of Jesus within their cultural setting. The central theme of the sermons of most African preachers concerned Jesus as the "messenger of God, Holy Spirit, and faith," manifested in prophecy, faith healing, the kingdom of God, and the need for repentance. In all these themes, emphasis was placed on the life, work, and resurrection of Jesus Christ. Contextually, missionaries did not know how to present this theological phenomenon to African Christians.

The point I seek to make is that Shona people did exactly the same thing Paul did in Romans: assign God or the Supreme Being greater eminence as the God of all peoples, nations, and races. God, the provider of all things, *Wedenga* ("the one from heaven") and *Wokumusoro* ("the one from above"), acquired greater significance in both individual and communal religious experiences of African Christians. The designation "African Christianity" offers the most acceptable title of Shona Christianity as a deliberate, constructed response from precolonial, colonial, and postcolonial Africans. In African Christianity, God was far more clearly defined than God ever was in the missionary faith. Practitioners of postcolonial Pauline theology seek to address the constructed identity of the colonized by the colonizers, and in so doing to interrogate and to reproduce such constructions in ways relevant to the culture of a people.

As a result of the Shona people's association with British colonizers and Euro-American missionaries, their identity was transformed to a great extent. Using the words of Homi Bhabha, the person who is colonized is a "hybridized" individual, and in most cases that individual has shifting identities. Hence, the response of Africans to Western Christianity was either mimicry or reconfiguration. Whether as African Christians or simply religious Africans, the arrival of Western influences aroused among the Shona people a new level of consciousness of identity and cultural configurations.

Third, and related to the two points made above, is the African theological notion that Jesus Christ needed to be proclaimed as the one crucified who took the curse of our sins upon himself. While Christology is at the center of the Christian message, missionaries presented a Jesus whose presence was exclusively Western. African theologians, however, came to discover that Jesus Christ cannot be a captive of one cultural group. While he communicates through the medium of culture, he is at the same time above culture.[17] In any case, through their own vernacular readings of the Bible, they came to know the truth that Jesus Christ was indeed God incarnate and superseded any and all forms of human limitation. As a higher ancestor, Jesus was believed to be present, working powerfully among his people and assisting them in their need, danger, and temptation.

Fourth, African Christians believed that this Jesus must be proclaimed as the one to come who will appear at the full revelation of God's kingdom. Missionaries talked about Jesus Christ in abstract terms, and yet, for Paul as well as for African-Christian believers, Christ is the heartbeat of faith and is viewed as healer and savior.

In my view, it is because God's word occupied such a central position in postcolonial African Christianity, and specifically its orientation to Paul's theology, that the church in Africa is usually labeled as authentically Pauline.[18] Thus colonial and postcolonial African Christians reconfigured the meaning of faith; especially in relation to colonizers, who had assumed an individualistic perception of God. Faith in postcolonial terms emerged as "Jesus faith"—his radical "Yes-Saying" to God with his whole life. Jesus' radical faithfulness revealed new possibilities of righteousness for all human beings—Jews and Greeks, and consequently British colonizers, missionaries, and the Shona people. In postcolonial Christianity, Jesus cannot be fully identified with that great religious phenomenon of the Western world known as missionary Christianity, nor can historical Christianity claim him as its exclusive possession. As an ancestor, Jesus belongs to all people, races, and nations.

Paul's Faith in Colonial and Postcolonial Context (Rom. 3:22—4:25)

Colonial and missionary interpretation focused entirely on the individual's quest for salvation. African Christians, with their new Pauline understanding of Jesus, saw faith in relational and communal terms. New Testament commentators should take notice of Rom. 3:22, where Paul says, "The righteousness of God through faith is *for all who believe*." It is crucial to notice also the collective pronoun in verse 23: "for *all* have sinned."[19] Here again a collective pronoun embraces the shortfall of all humanity, and Shona Christians interpreted this as a means through which relationships between enemies can be reconfigured into relationships of reconciliation and forgiveness. As a postcolonial reader, I propose that Western missionaries misunderstood Paul's concept of faith, a misunderstanding probably present in the twenty-first-century Christian church as well. This is reminiscent of Rudolf Bultmann's statement that "righteousness of God means that it is a gift which is conferred upon humanity on the basis of God's free grace alone. Thus, faith has Jesus Christ as the object, literally meaning the faith of Jesus Christ."[20] This understanding of God was opaque to colonial missionaries, partly because of their individualistic gospel and their denial of the formation of a diversified Christian community. Recently, Philip Esler in his exegesis has attempted a hermeneutical framework of interpersonal communication and communion, but this is not what Paul was about in Romans.[21] Rather, Paul envisaged a multiethnic faith community whose identity was marked by faith in the One who gave new life to Abraham and Sarah, regardless of their bodies, which were biologically beyond conceiving.

African Christians contextualized the center of Paul's theological thought not only as involving individual salvation but also as involving the benefits of Jesus' faithfulness. Brigitte Kahl comes close to African Christians' interpretation of faith. Commenting on Paul's Letter to the Galatians, she notes, "Faith emerges as a radical trust of and commitment to the other of God-in-Christ, and the other of the neighbor-foreigner."[22] Colonially and postcolonially, African Christians viewed their relationship with colonizers under the rubric of the love of Christ who gave himself on behalf of humanity (Gal. 2:20). Thus faith in postcolonial terms is viewed as a call to reconciliation with the former enemy who came to colonize and conquer. Again, the language of Romans supports the new understanding of the faith of Jesus Christ. In Rom. 4:12, Paul speaks of the "faith of our father Abraham," a reading that abolishes imperialistic readings of Romans and creates a "remnant community," similar to that which God called forth in Abraham.[23] The view of the "remnant" is well captured in the words of Giorgio Agamben, who argued, "But if man is that which may be infinitely destroyed, this also means that something other than this destruction, and within this destruction, remains and that man is this remnant."[24]

The idea of the remnant helps resolve tensions that have been rising over the years, especially with regard to Paul's advocating for a universal Christianity. My thesis is that the remnant eliminates any references to Paul's Abraham as the father of a spiritual people with a universal identity, transcending all particular identities, and substitutes instead the concept of Abraham's people as the remnant drawn from Jews and non-Jews. In Romans 9–11, Paul underscores the metaphor of a remnant (Rom. 11:1-10) of ethnic Jews who had come to believe in Jesus Christ and juxtaposes it with Gentiles who will later be part of the Jesus community. Theologically, this remnant language frames Paul's basic paradigm of what constitutes Christianity. In postcolonial terms, it can probably be called "multiethnic Christianity" in that it is contextually and widely diversified.

I contend that African Christians, with their exposure to and dialogue with Western Christianity, came to the realization that faith in Jesus Christ welcomes diversity and recognizes cultural differences. This is the genius of African Christianity: it has concern for all peoples, nations, ethnic/tribal races, and genders. Missionary Christianity, on the other hand, focused on leaving other races, tribes, and peoples alone, especially those who refused Western penetration into their tribal cultures. My reading of Paul in colonial and postcolonial contexts convinces me to begin thinking that the "new people," which comes into existence on the basis of the Messiah Jesus and with Abraham as the faith ancestor, is not a universal humanity that transcends and abolishes differences. Instead, the messianic calling eliminates this world's divisions and produces a remnant in which Jews and Greeks can no longer coincide with themselves. Thus what was "called forth" in Father Abraham is not a universal human being, but a remnant. The call of God takes Abraham away from his cradle, consequently constituting him as the spiritual and faith ancestor or progenitor of a remnant.

Paul exposes the logic of this remnant in Rom. 3:29. The story of the great faith patriarch, the archetype of God's people, is embedded in these words of Paul in Rom. 3:28–30: "For we maintain that a man is justified by faith apart from observing the law. Is God the God of Jews only? Is he not the God of Gentiles too? Yes, of Gentiles too, since there is only one God, who will justify the circumcised by faith and the uncircumcised through that same faith." Particularly striking was the agreement between the African worldview and that of Paul's Abraham. Almost immediately, the Western missionary's preaching of abstract faith was replaced with the African's existential understanding of faith. People like Abraham "the father of all the faithful" and Moses, Enoch, Rahab, Isaac, Jacob, and the entire ancestral roll in Heb. 11:1–39, became relevant for African Christians. Echoing Richard Hays, I claim that Paul's theological argument in Rom. 3:28–30 "invites all people, including Gentiles, into right relation with God through faith," an understanding that is analogous to what Shona biblical interpreters were doing during and after colonization.[25]

Perhaps of even greater importance than just reading about ancestors was that African Christians began to include hymns about the "faith of Abraham" in their worship services.[26] It should not be surprising that African Christians should have jumped to conclusions of this kind. Even today, the majority of literate African Christians are able to read the Bible in many languages including English, and the Bible is, in many cases, the only literature available to them. The translation of the Bible into the vernacular is also a factor in a new process of growing theological awareness: this hitherto unrecognized people is nevertheless important enough to have the word of God in their own language.

Vernacular readings and theological interpretations of the Bible assisted Africans to recognize that which was called out in Abraham was not the flesh. Rather, what was called out in Abraham was the "spirit," that which transcends race, culture, genealogy, gender, and ethnic differences. The point I seek to make is that vernacular hermeneutics utilizes both descriptive and prescriptive tasks in its approach to spirituality and faith. Descriptive approach describes and documents the actual encounter between Western Christianity and African traditional religion. In that encounter, indigenous people reconfigured Christianity in dynamic and pluralistic ways; and, in the process, they were able to be inclusive of all indigenous and ethnic voices. In opposition to the prescriptive task, indigenous Christian faith seeks to hear what the "word of God" is actually saying to them. Rather than a universal approach to Christianity, the uniqueness of indigenous African faith welcomes local people's questions of the Bible to hear what missionaries said about God and to use that as a prism to hear the unfamiliar. What in particular is God calling them to be in relation to ancestors of faith gone before (Heb. 11:1–39)? Thus African Christianity is a deliberate, constructed response to and engagement with what missionaries—because of their allegiance to an imperialistic heritage—failed to see in Paul. Using Daniel Boyarin's terms, that which Africans actively picked up and transformed through their own reading of Abraham was the image of androgyny that Paul argues for in his discussion of "no male and female" in Gal. 3:28. In other words, the image of Abraham in Romans 4 cannot be clearly understood if readers leave out Gen. 1:27: "So God created man in his own image, in the image of God he created him; male and female he created them."

Thus what was called forth from Abraham was the "spiritual remnant," the first human—male and female—of Genesis who was in everything a spiritual androgyne. African theologians have come to label this spiritual androgyne as *Ubuntu*, that is, the essence of a truly female and male human being. The fundamental point to be made is that in Abraham, God called forth the soul into a true relationship with the Creator. The soul's response to God unites it with its divine source and thereby achieves its immortality. In Philo's interpretation of Gen. 2:17, the notion is well framed in more spiritual terms, emphasizing the primal divine human being before the fall.[27]

The new language of Romans supports the new understanding of the faith of Jesus—faith that invites nations to transcend biological and racial boundaries. In explicit terms, Paul speaks of the nature of "the faith of our father Abraham" in a more inclusive theology that calls and invites all into the God of all peoples and nations. If Paul's concept of faith is that of a radical obedience, then Phil. 2:6–11 also supports this new understanding. For here Paul speaks clearly of Jesus' obedience to God in his human condition: "He humbled himself and became obedient up to the point of death, even death on the cross." Thus, in African-Christian terms, faith meant an act of surrender, or capitulation, to God in all areas of human life. Africans found appealing the new concept of Paul's language of Jesus' death and resurrection. It was Paul's conviction that Jesus' trust in God was so perfect that he gave his life itself as a gift. This is a powerful step away from imperialistic and colonial theology.

In postcolonial terms, Paul's Jesus gives God what imperialism does for itself. Thus Jesus' faith is the harbinger of God's imperium; it is the dawning revelation of the righteousness that Isaiah promised as light and salvation for the Gentiles (Isa. 58:8). This is what Shona Christians recognized in their reading and interpretation of Paul in Romans. It was this form of faith that missionaries misunderstood when they sought to convert Africans to Western Christianity.

While Paul's language was difficult for missionaries, African Christians were able to understand and appropriate his theology into their own context. Paul is at pains to theologize the death and resurrection of Jesus, and he carries this interpretation by drawing upon the language of Israel's cult. Among other areas of Romans, the following passage (3:25–26) was of great appeal to Africans: "God put [him] forward as a sacrifice of atonement by his blood, effective through faith. He did this to show his righteousness, because in his divine forbearance he had passed over the sins previously committed; it was to prove at the present time that he himself is righteous and that he justifies the one who has faith in Jesus." In Greco-Roman literature, "expiation or propitiation is that which serves as an instrument for regaining the goodwill of a deity—concretely, a means of propitiation or expiation, gift to procure expatiation."[28] The notion of the "mercy seat" resonated with Africans' understanding of the entire process of sacrifice through the shedding of blood either of a lamb or a bull.

Thus Paul's theologizing is so complete that he represents God as taking the initiative in removing the impediments to a relationship with God's self (3:25). Paul wants to argue that "God put him [Jesus] forward as a propitiation, through faith in his blood, for a demonstration of his righteousness on account of the passing over of former sins." This Pauline theology was intrinsically African, but missionaries had no concrete understanding of blood as a form of expiation. In other words, missionaries never bothered to understand the religion and the inner theological logic of African life; they were preoccupied with the crusade against "heathenism" and the aggressive assertion of white superiority.

The book of *4 Maccabees* makes a few analogous moves. In *4 Macc.* 6:27–28, the martyr Eleazar endures and suffers unto death. Just before being put to death, he cries out to God: "You know God that although I could save myself, I die in fiery torment for the sake of the law. Be merciful to your people, and let my punishment be a satisfaction on their behalf. Make my blood purification for them and take my life as a ransom for theirs." *Fourth Maccabees*

17:22 is the closest parallel to Paul's language about Jesus' death in Rom. 3:24–25: "And through the blood of those devout ones and their death as an atoning sacrifice, divine Providence preserved Israel that previously had been mistreated." In Shona culture, the analogy is very African because Mbuya Nehanda, the heroine who died by hanging at the hands of the British, said similar words, "propitiation and blood." It was through the blood of these righteous heroes and heroines and the propitiation through their death that divine providence saved Israel and consequently became a source of salvation for African Christians.

Abraham as Ancestor in African Context (Rom. 4:1–25)

In Romans 4, Paul links expiation and propitiation with Abraham's status as an ancestor of "all who believe" in God whose sins have been expiated by Christ's death and resurrection. This is an example of where missionaries lost the true meaning of evangelism in relation to winning the soul and heart of Africa. Their cultural imperialism displaced pure religious evangelism. The result of this cultural arrogance was that the most distinguished characteristic of missionary operations in Africa was their almost unanimous refusal to incorporate elements of Paul's theology into the African-Christian worldview. Yet African Christians were quick to contextualize and pursue religious evangelism along the lines of Jesus Christ, Paul, and Peter. In Pauline theology, God's righteousness represents the supreme expression of God's love and purpose, fully revealed in Christ Jesus. Thus grace and God's faithfulness were demonstrated in the atonement as the fulfillment of the covenant, and this was authentically African. In the death and resurrection of Jesus, salvation through faith was opened to all groups, even those who lacked qualifications.[29] Missionaries failed to see the implications of the death of Jesus as an event open to all people, nations, and races on the basis of faith. In Rom. 3:27–31, Paul affirms that God deals impartially with both Jews and Gentiles.

God's impartiality constitutes God's very integrity (justice, righteousness, and covenantal loyalty), which exists apart from the law (Rom. 3:21).[30] Although the term *righteousness* does not appear in Romans 4, its theological imprint is evident. Arguing from a Jewish contextual theology, especially Gen. 15:6, Paul addresses the nature and purposes of God as fulfilled in the calling forth of Abraham as the ancestor/forefather of all nations (Gen. 12:1–2). Thus Abraham becomes the formative figure in fulfilling the creative plan of God and, consequently, opening a door to all future faith believers. While Jews of Paul's period would have looked at Abraham from a biological perspective, Paul, who now believes in the expiational blood of Jesus retrospectively, views Abraham as "father of us all" who share his faith (Rom. 4:16) and follow in the footsteps of faith. Paul contends that the righteousness attributed to Abraham was written for those who believe in the Lord Jesus, "who was given for our transgressions and raised for our justification" (Rom. 4:25). Missionaries did not see Paul's theology as one of a communal nature, but only individual in nature. Therefore, missionaries did not practice biblical Christianity, but a colonial religion in which African and missionary relations were set at odds between inferiors and superiors, consequently destroying the family collectivity of African culture.

In a succinct theological formulation, Paul addresses the question of Rom. 4:1—in relation to the status of Abraham as a father according to the flesh—by separating Abraham from the perspective of the flesh and placing him in another realm, that of faith and spirit. What Abraham founded was not an individual nation, but a new ethnos of brothers and sisters related to God on the basis of faith. Stanley Stowers argues that Abraham serves as a model not of the believer's faith but rather of how God brings to pass God's promises by founding lineages that incorporate whole peoples into the blessings made possible by founding ancestors.[31] This perspective is inadequate in that it does not address the complementary roles of God and Abraham: a quality that Africans found to be relevant in their belief in God and Jesus Christ. At every moment during the encounter of God and Abraham, as well as God's encounter with Sarah, we see a God who is always in communion with creation and in dialogue with humanity.[32]

From an African point of view, Abraham's faith/trust is the central aspect of his ancestry, a quality that Paul takes pains to explain in Rom. 4:1–25. Here is a faith, Paul explains, that is not loyalty to one's cultural superiority or to an imperial figure, but rather loyalty to the God of Abraham. In arguing this perspective for the figure of Abraham, Paul thus describes his present life in Christ Jesus and, consequently, invites others to do the same. His conversion to Christianity is now a paradigm for all future Christians. Paul juxtaposes faith and grace as theological terms operative in the calling of Abraham. This grace, according to Paul, exemplified itself in Abraham, who, in his ungodliness, received God's promises without working to earn them. Abraham simply believed this gracious offer, and it was reckoned or counted to him as a gift of righteousness.

Thus, because of his faith, Abraham becomes the "honorific parent of all believers, explicitly including those unconnected to his physical lineage."[33] Philo also depicted Abraham as the prototype of faith, thus taking over the Jewish tradition that regarded the patriarch as "our Father κατὰ σάρκα" ("according to the flesh"). Here again, though Paul is operating within the same context, he moves out of that context by making Abraham the ancestor of the Christian faith as well.[34] Analogous to African traditional religion is the notion of "kinship" present in Paul's discussion of Abraham. The privileged position of the Jews and Gentile proselytes is no longer a thing to boast about. Similarly, the ingrained cultural nationalism of the missionaries was challenged by African preachers who sought Christianity on the basis of equality. Ethnocentricism was definitely one strong characteristic of missionaries who described Africans as the "degraded descendants of Ham," "kaffirs," "natives," and even "niggers,"[35] all of which were then racist, derogatory, and arrogant terms unfit for one Christian to use toward another. A true apostle and messenger of God ought to have been able to rise above bigotry, prejudice, and discrimination.

Paul does just this in Rom. 4:1–25: he moves Abraham beyond the earlier Jewish way of talking about Abraham as a symbol of national identity. In this respect, Paul preached love and the kinship of all peoples as propounded by Jesus Christ and the apostles. The death and resurrection of Jesus have brought about something new; now all people who have the faith of Abraham are able to cross boundaries of institutionalized hate and caste system and live together as human beings accountable to God. Like any other great ancestor, their stories are told and retold, so Paul turns to the question of "when," thus helping his Jewish Christians to comprehend the plan of God. Here circumcision comes into play, not as the mark of the faith relation, but as a seal—a reminder of the relationship between God and Abraham. The narrative context of Gen. 15:6 and 17:5 takes center stage in Paul's theology of Abraham. God's appointment of Abraham was before circumcision, and that takes away the ethnocentric pride of those who claim circumcision to be the definitive mark of identification with Abraham. Philo of Alexandria, who was a contemporary of Paul, also goes to pains to explain the role and call of Abraham as an ancestor of faith. Philo wants readers to see beyond the individual Abraham and to understand the spirit that was called forth, or the "remnant," out of Abraham. Here then is an inkling of how Jesus' surrender could be redemptive for others. Jesus' active surrender forges a new relationship between humanity and God on the basis of faith.

In similar fashion, Abraham is called God's friend, not in a passive form, but in an active sense (*he who loves me*).[36] The relationship between the righteousness of God as God's present saving action for Israel and Israel's election in Abraham is even stronger in Isa. 51:1–8. The narrative of Paul's argument raises two issues. First, God acted righteously not only toward the historical Abraham but also toward future generations. Second, emphasis should not be placed on Abraham's merits or works but on the free grace of God—the righteousness of God given to the believing children of Abraham. Thus Paul's gospel (Rom. 1:16-17) opens grace and salvation to outsiders, and Paul views his message as the consummation of God's promises. Africans were quick to identify the same understanding of the nature and role of the gospel as an offering of God's salvation. Missionaries, however, preached a different gospel; theirs was about championing their race, their culture, and their wealth as the instruments of God's divine will and order. The preaching of Christian faith as repentance, salvation, good works, and afterlife in heaven was no longer an end in itself, as it had been for Jesus, Paul, Stephen, and Peter—the greatest missionaries in Christianity.

The appropriation of Abraham among Shona Christians opened new theological windows, especially around the concepts of faith and grace. Thus what Abraham merited for later-believing generations was pure grace. In postcolonial contexts, grace eliminated imperial pride, prejudice, and racial superiority and thus helped colonizers relate to Shona Christians as brothers and sisters. Just as faith and belief placed Abraham in a covenant relationship with God, so Africans saw themselves as equal beneficiaries of this relationship. Abraham represented many qualities with which Africans were able to relate. For example, Abraham was a great wanderer, moving from Ur to Haran, Schechem, Bethel, Egypt, and Hebron.[37] Not only could Shona Christians identify with his lifestyle, but Abraham's character also provided an ideal. Abraham was a victorious warrior who sat with kings (Genesis 14) and a mighty prince (Genesis 23); he was hospitable to strangers (Genesis 18) and a prophet who interceded for others (Genesis 18, 20). Africans, too, had similar heroes and heroines who did similar acts, thus resembling Abraham's story of ancestorship. The most important aspect about Abraham was the promise he received. He was "assigned the role of a mediator of blessing in God's saving plan, for 'all the families of the earth'"[38] (Gen. 12:1-3). It is clear that Abraham's promises take on multicultural dimensions and give rise to a well-developed apologetic formulated not only for Gentiles but also for future believing nations.

Faith and grace as they operated in Abraham had an equalizing force. In Romans 9–11, Paul argues for a theology of grace that abolishes all racial and ethnic divisions and unites all believing nations to Jesus Christ (Rom. 9:24; 10:12). In colonial terms, both colonizers and colonized are summoned to a new form of relationship based on faith, love, and reconciliation. Paul's Abraham in Romans abolished imperial claims to power, as manifested in the ministry, death, and resurrection of Jesus Christ. In a context where both Africans and colonialists had become enemies, Pauline theology became a resource for allowing relations to be formulated not on the basis of power but on what Jesus Christ did on the cross. In constructing an alternative world based on faith and grace in Romans 9–11, Paul destroys the mythological universe of imperial rule, thereby assisting readers to view the emperor's real status—clay in the potter's hands (Rom. 9:14-21) and a servant appointed by God (Rom. 13:4). Thus, in colonial context, Africans saw Paul's God as one whom they had already known and believed in—"Father Abraham," whom they had sung about in both academic and Sunday school settings.

For colonized and postcolonial African Christians, Paul became a resource through whom they could enter God's family and have the privilege to call God "Abba, Father"—Jesus' intimate address of God (Mark 14:36). As a forgiven and forgiving family, Shona Christians considered themselves to be incorporated into a new family by grace (Rom. 10:12; 11:5-6). Hence, a postcolonial Christianity is possible, one in which the grace of Jesus Christ is operative (Rom. 5:17, 20; 2 Cor. 4:15; 8:7; 9:8). Thus the central thrust of Pauline postcolonial Christianity is an affirmation that on the basis of faith all can claim the God of Abraham. This God was obscured not only by the Enlightenment but also by colonial missionaries. Like an awakening, African Christians realized that the God whom they had believed before the advent of colonialism and missionary enterprise was the very God about whom Paul was theologizing in Romans, particularly with regard to the oneness of God and God's impartial treatment of all peoples (Rom. 3:27-31). What needs to be noted here, from a postcolonial perspective, is that the God of Abraham has discernible aspects. First, God's relationship with Abraham was not imperialistic in nature but was complementary: a relationship of reciprocity. After receiving and accepting the call and promise of God, Abraham wandered under divine protection, trusting only in God, and came to a land where he established a new ethnos whose identity was based on faith.

Abraham's God is also a down-to-earth God, one who actively seeks to have a relationship with peoples on the basis of trust and faith (Gen. 18:16-32). Thus the God of Abraham is not an imperialistic figure or dominating power; instead, God invites human participation and is not far away but accessible, as well as approachable, by all. God's interaction with Hagar (Gen. 16:7-14) and Abimelech (Gen. 20:3-6), both outsiders, exhibits a quality that appealed to African Christians who had grown accustomed to imperial modes of segregation and arrogance. The promise to Abraham and Sarah was encompassed with a blessing and the presence of the divine (Gen. 12:1-3; 17:7-8, 16). In an interesting declaration, God declares an oath to Abraham, saying, "I will be God to you and to your descendants after you" (Gen. 17:7-8).

If this postcolonial reading of Romans is correct, then, of course, it can be said that Paul's theology in this epistle was obscured by both missionaries and colonialists, and one can begin to comprehend his creative construction of Abraham in the Greco-Roman period of Augustus. In Rom. 3:21—4:25, Paul highlights the nature of God as a God of impartiality and his example of Abraham as an ancestor of faith, thus countering the ideological claims of the empire. Africans did the same thing, incorporating and appropriating Abraham's promises and faith into their African Christianity and thus preparing them for a postcolonial faith community. Understanding Romans in this fashion has revolutionary implications for New Testament readers who are keen to contextualize the essential Christian message to the global world. In chapter 4, I will juxtapose Aeneas and Abraham in an effort to help New Testament readers appreciate possibilities of contextualizing Paul's theology of Abraham's faith and spirituality and, consequently, to see the usefulness of Pauline exegesis in postcolonial contexts.

Notes

1. The idea and logic of a powerful ancestry is described in Erich S. Gruen, *Culture and National Identity in Republican Rome* (Ithaca, NY: Cornell University Press, 1992), 6–51. See also Deut. 26:5, "And you shall make response before the Lord your God, 'A wandering Aramean was my father. And he went down into Egypt and sojourned there, few in number, and there he became a nation, great, mighty, and populous.'"

2. Gruen, *Culture and National Identity*, 20–21.

3. D. E. Needham, E. K. Mashingaidze, and N. Bhebe, eds., *From Iron Age to Independence: A History of Central Africa* (Harare, Zimbabwe: Longman, 1991), 129. See also chap. 1, pp. 1–2, above.

4. The word *myth* is used in this book to refer to stories that matter to a community, one that is told and retold because it has significance for one generation after another, both politically and religiously.

5. For a detailed discussion of the role of ancestors, readers should consult Davina C. Lopez, *Apostle to the Conquered: Reimagining Paul's Mission* (Minneapolis: Fortress Press, 2008), 153–63; and Neil Elliott, *The Arrogance of Nations: Reading Romans in the Shadow of the Empire* (Minneapolis: Fortress Press, 2008), 121–38. What is missing in these two authors, however, is a clear context that juxtaposes Aeneas and Abraham and examines how that context assisted Paul in his creative reconstruction of reconfiguration of Abraham as spiritual ancestor of a multitude of nations, peoples, and races. They both ignore the colonial and postcolonial context, and that is the uniqueness of my theological discovery: the role of Abraham in the Shona people's invocation of Nehanda as a spiritual, religious, and political female heroine.

6. The designation "African Christianity" is used in this book to refer to a Christian community founded by once-colonized Africans and serving the theological needs of Africans.

7. The theological notion of "the impartial righteousness of god" is well elaborated in Robert Jewett, *Romans: A Commentary* (Minneapolis: Fortress Press, 2007), 148–91.

8. See chap. 1, p. 14 above.

9. D. Western, *The Value of the African Past: The International Review of Missions* (London: Oxford University Press, 1926), 418–19.

10. See Canaan Banana, "The Case for a New Bible," in *Rewriting the Bible: The Real Issues*, ed. I. Mukonyora and F. J. Verstraele (Gweru, Zimbabwe: Mambo Press, 1993), 17–32.

11. See William S. Campbell, *Paul's Gospel in an Intercultural Context: Jew and Gentile in the Letter to the Romans* (New York: Peter Lang, 1992), 26–29.

12. While the notion of boasting is explained in Jewett, *Romans*, 296, it is not given a colonial context. Boasting in African religious perspective involves elevation of one's superiority at the expense of others who are powerless in terms of politics, economy, and social standing.

13. See N. T. Wright, *The Resurrection of the Son of God* (Minneapolis: Fortress Press, 2003), 242–49.

14. M. L. Daneel, *Quest for Belonging: Introduction to a Study of African Independent Churches* (Gweru, Zimbabwe: Mambo Press, 1987), 189–91.

15. Ibid., 180.

16. See M. F. C. Bourdillon, ed., *Christianity South of the Zambezi* (Gweru, Zimbabwe: Mambo Press, 1977), 2:43–44.

17. See H. Richard Niebuhr, *Christ and Culture* (New York: Harper, 1956), 129.

18. Marshall W. Murphree, *Christianity and the Shona* (Gweru, Zimbabwe: Mambo Press, 1969).

19. Emphasis added.

20. Rudolf Bultmann, *Theology of the New Testament* (New York: Scribner, 1951), 1:285.

21. Philip Esler, *New Testament Theology: Communion and Community* (Minneapolis: Fortress Press, 2005), 273–82.

22. Brigitte Kahl, *Galatians Re-Imagined: Reading with the Eyes of the Vanquished* (Minneapolis: Fortress Press, 2010), 280–81.

23. The word *remnant* is used in this book to refer to that which God called for in Abraham, a paradoxical spirit that goes back to the creation of the ideal human being.

24. Giorgio Agamben, *The Time That Remains: A Commentary on the Letter to the Romans* (Stanford: Stanford University Press, 2005), 53.

25. See Richard B. Hays, *Echoes of Scripture in the Letters of Paul* (New Haven: Yale University Press, 1989), 54–55.

26. For a detailed hymn on the faith of ancestors, see *Ngoma dze United Methodist Church Ye Zimbabwe, or Hymns of the United Methodist Church in Zimbabwe* (Harare, Zimbabwe: United Methodist Press, 1964), 188. The specific hymn is no. 187. Here the hymn even mentions Paul's faith (*Ngerutendo Rukuru*), thus helping readers to see the contextualization of Paul and Abraham in colonial and postcolonial contexts.

27. See Philo's interpretation of Gen. 2:17 in Daniel Boyarin, *A Radical Jew: Paul and the Politics of Identity* (Berkeley: University of California Press, 1997), 187–88.

28. Walter Bauer, *Greek –English Lexicon of the New Testament and Other Early Christian Literature*, ed. William Arndt, F. Wilbur Gingrish, and Frederick W. Danker, 3rd ed. (Chicago: University of Chicago Press, 2000).

29. Ibid.

30. See Dieter Georgi, *Theocracy in Paul's Praxis*, trans. Davil L. Green (Minneapolis: Fortress Press, 1991), 17–18, 79–97.

31. Stanley Kent Stowers, *A Rereading of Romans: Justice, Jews and Gentiles* (New Haven: Yale University Press, 1994), 8-9.

32. See Gen. 18:1-2, 16-32. See also Michael E. Stone, trans., *The Testament of Abraham: The Greek Recensions* (Missoula, MT: Society of Biblical Literature, 1972), 2–23.

33. Jewett, *Romans*, 307.

34. See Ernst Kasemann, *Perspectives on Paul* (Philadelphia: Fortress, 1971), 79.

35. See Edwin Monk, ed., *Dr. Livingstone's Cambridge Lectures* (1858; repr., Farnborough, UK: Gregg International, 1968), 170 (February 15, 1859).

36. *1 Clement* 10.1–7.

37. Dieter Georgi, *Die Gegner des Paulus im 2. Korntherbrief* (Assen: Neukirchener, 1964). The suggestion here is that Jews of the Diaspora would have identified with Abraham as the original wanderer. Shona people had similar experiences because of their displacement from their traditional land and homes by British colonialists.

38. Gerhard von Rad, *Genesis: A Commentary* (London: SCM, 1972), 160.

4

Aeneas—A Constructed Ancestor

In the overarching story of the last three chapters, I have discussed issues of power, ancestry, and religious identity during and after colonial domination. Focusing on the power of ancestors, this chapter will consider the construction and reinvention of Aeneas as an ancestor of both Greeks and Romans of the Augustan era. Chapter 5 will then focus on the juxtaposition of Aeneas and Abraham and how this comparison is useful in the exegesis and theology of Paul in colonial and postcolonial African contexts. While both figures represent marginalization from their beginning, their stories are a perfect fit to Paul's theology of a God who "chose what is foolish in the world to shame the wise."[1] Descent from a powerful ancestor has always held great appeal for many nations throughout history. The particular meaning attached to founders—especially by Romans and Jews of the Diaspora—is an important paradigm for interpreting biblical texts. The story of Abraham, for example, was told and enhanced by such writers as the Hellenistic Jewish philosopher Philo and the Romano-Jewish historian and hagiographer Josephus. Their works were greatly appreciated by readers in the Roman Empire of the Augustan period.

To the Jews of the Diaspora, Abraham symbolized crucial aspects of that Jewish experience. He was the great wanderer, moving from Ur to Haran, Shechem, Bethel, Egypt, and Hebron.[2] Not only could Diaspora Jews identify with his seemingly unsettled lifestyle; his character also provided an ideal. The Epistle to the Romans was addressed to an audience composed of not only Jews but Greeks and Romans as well.

Virgil's *Aeneid*, written in praise of the cultural and moral renewal program of Augustus (63 BCE–19 CE), is indeed a story about Aeneas, the ancestor of both Greeks and Romans. Virgil (70–19 BCE) wrote in a period of identity crisis for the Roman Empire. Critical scholarship documents that religious and cultural identity was at its lowest level, and Augustus embarked on a program of renewal and reestablishment of the empire's distinctiveness. The emphasis was once more on ancestors as signifiers of Rome's identity and power in the world. What is happening in the *Aeneid* is of fundamental significance because Virgil's aim in writing of the founding of Greeks and Romans was to define the empire's moral and religious identity. His ideological aim was to inspire Rome's inhabitants with a divine identity stretching from Aeneas and, consequently, embodied in the golden age of the Augustan era.[3]

It is my contention that when Paul wrote Romans, he was aware of the importance that Greeks and Romans attached to Aeneas as a founding ancestor. In fact, the construction of Abraham as an ancestor of faith begins in his letter to the churches of Galatia, where those converts would have been familiar with ancestors.[4] The apostle's audience would have been familiar with the traditions around Aeneas as a culturally, politically, and ideologically constructed ancestor of the Roman Empire.[5] Thus, while it may seem controversial to assert that Paul's theology should be understood in the context of the reconciliation of Greeks and Romans, and the values and people who claim Aeneas as an ancestor, the evidence of that insight is beyond doubt. It is likely that my assertion of the Aeneas-Abraham paradigm is a novel one in the exegesis and theological commentary of Paul within African Christianity. The Paul proclaimed by colonial missionaries was largely European in orientation, with emphasis on the universal aspects of his thought and with a disregard for cultural adaptations. Even American missionaries who later came to Africa adopted the same Eurocentric Paul, and the gospel they preached was basically on individualism—a distinctively American interpretation of Romans.

Africans are a community-oriented people, and their vernacular readings of Paul helped them grasp the apostle's message of equality of all creatures before an impartial God (Gal. 2:6; Rom. 3:29–30). The story of Paul's Jesus fascinated the Shona people, and it became the foundation story of a new people. The story was also connected to founding ancestors, namely, the celebration of ritualized meals closely tied to ancestors. Paul's Epistle to the Romans, especially his creative theology around the construction of Abraham as an ancestor of *all* faith peoples, was generative among Shona Christians, who in their response to the gospel of Jesus Christ considered themselves to be legitimate beneficiaries of the promises made to Abraham.

On what basis can once-colonized African Christians claim descent from Abraham? The crucial aspect of the Aeneas-Abrahamic ancestry becomes foundational as a paradigm for comprehending the Shona people's affinity to Paul's construction of Abraham, allowing indigenous people to creatively appropriate selected aspects of British Christianity into their culture and, consequently, into postcolonial African Christianity. Diaspora Jews and inhabitants of Rome were shaped by and imbued with religion and ideology. The former would be firm adherents of Abraham as an ancestor on the basis of biological descent; the latter would be stamped by a politically constructed view of the tradition of Aeneas. Rome, to which Paul's epistle was addressed, not only was the capital of the Roman Empire but also was seen as the capital of the Mediterranean world and its neighboring areas. Indeed, during the time of Paul, Rome was the center of the Caesar religion, established throughout the empire. Evidence for Rome's religious and cultural world is found not only in ancient literature but also in the New Testament, especially in the Acts of the Apostles, which depicts similar traditions.[6]

Christian communities in the Roman Empire were probably quick to identify with Paul's construction of Abraham in a context in which reverence of ancestors was common. Now I argue that Paul, recognizing the cultural and religious significance of ancestors in his own Jewish and Greco-Roman context, appropriated Abraham in much the same way that Augustus had appropriated Aeneas. Western New Testament scholarship, coming from the dominant colonial culture, has not adequately appreciated the significance of Romans 4 for African Christianity. The Shona experience of colonization helps readers recognize Paul's appeal to Abraham as a counter to the *Aeneid.* For the Shona people, the appeal to Abraham would counter Cecil Rhodes's claim to be the founder and ancestor of Zimbabwe. Likewise, Paul opposed the dominant, imperial ancestry of his day with Abraham. The following section will briefly offer a comparison of both Aeneas and Abraham and then present a dialectical view of Paul's elevation of Abraham as an above-and-beyond ancestor of faith for all faith peoples. The comparison will assist readers both in Africa and the world to faithfully and spiritually appropriate the exegesis of Paul in contexts where ancestors are highly regarded.

Aeneas in the Greco-Roman Empire of Augustus's Era

The period of Augustus was given prominence for its attachment to the Aeneas story and cult. Virgil, the Augustan poet, composed the *Aeneid* as both story and poem that would trace the divine origins of Rome from Aeneas the Trojan. The Aeneas story would eventually become one of reconciliation and friendship between both Greeks and Romans. Ideologically, the *Aeneid* later became the ideal Greco-Roman national epic that would serve the Julio-Claudian family well. In Greco-Roman antiquity, the constitutional elements of a community were connected with the telling of the founders, the *maiores.* In periods of war and social upheaval, ancestors as living traditions can be lost. As models of virtue and wisdom, Virgil's work was a retelling of a story, recasting and restating the tradition in ever-newer versions, thus making the *Aeneid* into a canon for the empire. In a different but similar fashion, Marianne Palmer Bonz has analyzed this story masterfully and instructively in her book *The Past as Legacy*.[7]

The journeys and wanderings of Aeneas, especially as a sacred story of establishing a new nation, are closely analogous to the stories of Abraham in Genesis 12–22. As Virgil retells the story of Rome's mythical past, his aim is to create an ideological statement that will be both convincing and acceptable to all Hellenes as a people with a sacred past.[8] It is a story of self-definition based on a powerful pedigree, similar to what Philo and Josephus wrote about Abraham. The story of Aeneas as canonized and retold in the context of the Roman Empire established an ideological view of Aeneas as a reconciling ancestor. The Augustan propaganda firmly revised and established the role and function of Aeneas and placed the Trojan as the ancestor of both Greeks and Romans. The celebration of Aeneas arose during the time of Augustus, through which a new narrative of Rome with the beginning of a new age was proclaimed. The celebration of Aeneas was not inclusive of all peoples within the empire, but was designed to benefit the political leaders of the Julio-Claudian family.[9]

The Roman state needed to be revived and transformed as an empire whose hegemony was to encompass the entire world. Therefore, the Greek historian and teacher of rhetoric Dionysius of Halicarnassus (c. 60 BCE–after 7 BCE) and Virgil saw it as their mission to provide both Greeks and Romans with a glorious autochthony, one that would birth a new kinship. These Roman intellectual writers of the Augustan age began to propagate the myth of Aeneas as a migrant hero who wandered from the ruins of Troy with the promise to form gods to establish a powerful new ethnos that would rule the universe.[10] Thus the two writers of the Augustan age who reshaped the Aeneas story had one ambition: namely, to make the hero a symbol of reconciliation between Greeks and Romans.

Ancestor Reconciliation

In periods of colonial and local wars, people turn to founding figures as symbols of identity and reconciliation. For Greeks and Romans, the story of Aeneas was socially, religiously, and politically constructed in order to forge a new identity.[11] Thus the role of Aeneas during the period of Augustus was well established as a story of power, ancestry, and new identity. There would be no way that Paul and his Roman audience could have ignored this deep-seated longing for a sense of identity rooted in ancestors. After all, Christianity and its rapid growth happened during this period of Rome's ascendancy under the leadership of Augustus. By the time Virgil wrote his poem, Aeneas was already venerated as the hero and founder of the greater part of the city-states in Italy, Sicily, and the northern Aegean.[12] While they did not like Greeks, the Romans desperately needed Greek intelligence and cooperation for the success of the empire. Therefore, both Greeks and Romans had to agree on the reconstruction of their identity, one that would see the collaboration of both nations. The myth assisted in shaping Rome as a distinctive, powerful empire whose foundations were now embedded in Trojan history.

In the construction of Aeneas as a reconciling figure, the legend was manipulated with international diplomatic insights, strengthening Rome's power within the Mediterranean world of Paul's audience. Thus Virgil's Aeneas was raised to a religious divinity. Rome, the place to which the last extended letter of Paul is addressed, was not only the capital of the Roman Empire and its neighboring areas, but was also the center of the Caesar religion that was firmly established on the basis of the Aeneas myth. Literature from the second century BC shows that Aeneas was worshiped as *pater indiges* or as *god* Aeneas, which means that the cult of Aeneas was well under way during the time of Augustus and consequently Paul's time.[13] The myth and cult of Aeneas helped to shape the empire's image in the context of a diversified culture. In postcolonial perspectives, the glorification of personal heroes and founders as bearers of national ideals and aspirations are both culturally and ideologically powerful. In essence, the praise of the Aeneas legend raised patriotic pride at the expense of other, less-powerful traditions and cultures of the Roman world.

In the ancient world, the construction of an ancestor was not a new phenomenon but was widely accepted as a way to restate traditions in ever-newer versions to the extent of canonization, as well as constitution. Most likely, Asia Minor as a whole was well aware of the erection of Augustus's temple and the establishment of a priesthood, all in the name of Aeneas's powerful ideology. I contend that twenty-first-century New Testament interpretation has until now not taken sufficient notice of the fact that the gospel of Augustus, namely, the tablet of *Res Gestae Divi Augusti* ("the deeds of the divine Augustus") is not only a political document but also clearly a theological document that would have been encountered by Paul and read by him in the cities of Asia Minor.[14] Indeed, public places and arenas in Pompeii would have had public displays of Augustus's propaganda.

In Pompeii, the Augustus temple still stands today, a fact that has not been taken into account when interpreters read Paul's Letter to the Romans.[15] In cases like these, readers are encountered with rituals and narratives through which founding ancestors are claimed and celebrated. The divine origins of Rome and Greece are well established in the works of Virgil, who wrote the following:

> Arma virumque cano, Troiae qui primus ab oris Italiam fato
> profugus Laviniaque venit litora—multum ille et terris iactatus
> et alto vi superum, saevae memorem Iunonis obi ram, multa quoque
> et bello passus, dum conderet urbem inferretque deos Latio; genus
> unde Latinum Albanique patres atque altae moenia Romae.[16]
>
> (Arms, and the man I sing, who, forc'd by fate,
> And haughty Juno's unrelenting hate,
> Expell'd and exil'd, left the Trojan shore.
> Long labors, both by sea and land, he bore,
> And in the doubtful war, before he won
> The Latian realm, and built the destin'd town;
> His banish'd gods restor'd to rites divine,
> And settled sure succession in his line,
> From whence the race of Alban fathers come,
> And the long glories of majestic Rome.)[17]

This is the story of creation, written by Virgil, whose task was to create the national epic of Rome's sacred foundation. The epic is analogous to the Exodus narrative, in which the story of Israel is narrated in sacred form. Augustus celebrated the stories of Aeneas's building an Altar of Peace—the *Ara Pacis*—where the depiction of the Trojan hero Aeneas was made visible.[18]

It is noteworthy that during the Hellenistic period of Augustus, the impulse to assert and glorify national heroes was expressed by elevating the character and history of founding fathers whose role included the unity of diverse cultural groups. In his program of restoration of the Republic, Augustus emphasized central elements of "renewal of religion and custom, *virtus*, and honor of the Roman people."[19] All this was ritualized in images that were visible in all public buildings. Roman historians and orators of this time were eager to show Rome's place in history as predestined by the gods and that its history in the decades to come would embrace the entire universe. In this sense, Aeneas is similar to Jewish heroes such as Moses, Abraham, and Daniel; and Aeneas's calling is very similar to the call of the Jewish founder. This theme will be addressed in the following pages, but for now it suffices to note that Aeneas was indeed a reconciling ancestor—and his status in history is analogous to that of Abraham.

The myth of Aeneas as a founding and reconciling ancestor was not only documented by Virgil and Dionysius of Halicarnassus but was also popularized by Roman scholars of the fifth century BCE.[20] In order for the empire to function, Romans sought to collaborate with Latin cities such as Lavinium and Alba Longa, whose claims to Trojan ancestry were well entrenched.[21] Here again, Aeneas is reconfigured as a symbol of reconciliation, collaboration, and friendship. Claiming descent from Aeneas worked well for the Romans, who would later exploit the figure in establishing firm imperial rule. In the end, the Aeneas myth served the Julio-Claudian dynasty by establishing a political ideology that would be used for the exploitation of the universe. Whether it was a construction or a myth, the story of Aeneas was later retold in a more vivid way by eyewitnesses of the Augustan era—namely, Dionysius of Halicarnassus and Virgil.

In the writings of Dionysius, Rome's origins were not only through Greeks but also through divine sanction, an aspect that would help the public to appreciate the empire's claim to divine mandate. Dionysius had one single aim—to construct Trojans in a Greek mold, whose migration from Asia to the Peloponnese was by divine fate.[22] When Aeneas landed in Italy, he was confronted by King Latinus, who had decided to make war with Aeneas's people. In defense of the whole band, Aeneas stepped forward and declared that he and all his people were wandering natives of Troy, who had come to Greece in obedience to the commands of the gods. The events after saw Aeneas accepted as a Greek citizen and extended a hand of fellowship by King Latinus. The story again is one of reconciliation between two powerful cultures and the creation of a new, shared identity based on the spirit of friendship. Thus Dionysius had one ambition—to construct Aeneas into a sacred ancestor of two ideologically oriented cultures. His language of ancestor construction resonates with Paul's construction of Abraham in Rom. 4:1-25, a text written probably in the context of Rome's audience, people who were familiar with ancestors.

The consideration of Rome's origins rooted in Trojan legends moves readers to appreciate the nation's allegiance to *pietas*—the principle of remembering the divine origins of Rome. *Pietas* was not just a virtue or a sign embodied on the Roman shields—it was "one of the most important leitmotifs of the Augustan era."[23] The origin of the concept dates back to the time when Aeneas rescued his father and *penates* ("sacred objects") from the sack of Troy.[24] Thus Aeneas's rescue of the Trojan *penates* was an act of preserving the divine history on which the narrative of the Roman state was based. Virgil's reconstruction of the past served Augustus's project of cultural renewal in which stories of the gods were retold in images erected in and around the Roman Empire. The ancestors, or *maiores*, remained, as before, models of virtue and wisdom, which the present should imitate in either stories or images.[25] Augustus did not allow the past to slip away, but rather he sought to revive it in such a way that it would be present in the living memory of all Roman citizens, consequently making tradition a philosophical justification for religious and political beliefs.

Karl Galinsky argues that "the Lavinian Penates were Trojanized and connected with Aeneas, and thus came to be considered the ancestral gods of Rome."[26] In this sense, a shared history, or myth of origin, becomes a key ingredient in defining a sense of identity. When political leaders invoke the ancestors, the goal is to provide justification for a stable model of legitimacy, one that would authenticate a nation's rule over others who do not share the same past. Augustus was focused on the issue of the *mos maiorum*, or the traditions of the ancestors, as the accepted Roman way, and reading Paul's Epistle to the Romans should remind readers that the Roman identity was fixed and known. Dionysius wrote an entire tractate dedicated to the religious and political significance of Lavinium and Alba Longa.[27] The Latin people erected hero shrines in honor of their founding ancestors.[28] As a major political leader in the redefinition of identity, Augustus exploited the issue of the Aeneas ancestry to his advantage and managed to build a more stable empire. Temples containing Trojan gods were erected in the Roman world, and, for Paul, it was clearly readable, understandable, and impossible to overlook.

Dionysius records the following illuminating inscription found in one of the temples:

> εἰς πόλιν ἣν κτίζῃσθα θεοῖς σέβας ἄφθιτον αἰεὶ
> θεῖναι, καὶ φυλακαῖς τε σέβειν θυσίαις τε χοροῖς τε.
> ἔστ' ἂν γὰρ τάδε σεμνὰ καθ' ὑμετέρην χθόνα μίμνῃ
> δῶρα Διὸς κούρης ἀλόχῳ σέθεν, ἡ δὲ πόλις σοι
> ἔσται ἀπόρθητος τὸν ἀεὶ χρόνον ἤματα πάντα.
>
> (In the town thou buildest worship undying found
> To gods ancestral; guard them. Sacrifice, Adore
> with choirs. For whilst these holy things in thy
> Land remain, Zeus' daughter's gifts of old
> Bestowed upon thy spouse, secure from harm

Thy city shall abide forevermore.)[29]

While the poem has nothing to do with Aeneas, its elements assist readers to appreciate how the veneration of ancestors was well established within the traditions of both Greeks and Romans. It was a consciously willed creation by both Rome's cultural guardians and politicians. Each feature of Rome's life—public, private, political, legal, religious, military, and domestic—had an aura of ancestral veneration.[30]In other writings, Aeneas was worshiped, venerated, and ritualized at Lavinium as *Indeges, pater Indeges*, or *Jupiter Indeges*.[31]

This sort of rhetorical deployment of the ancestors generates a picture of the past that resides in the memory of the living—it is a past that is fluid and without boundaries. Dionysius's ambition was to sustain the image of Aeneas as a prudent and virtuous ancestor, consequently making him a central religious figure within the political worldview of the Roman Empire. Political, cultural, and religious identities invested in the figure of Aeneas leads into an appreciation of the role of the divinity that guided ancestors—especially Aeneas and Abraham.

Virgil and the Ambivalnce of *Pietas*/*Fides*/Faith

The ways in which I have distinguished the character of Aeneas as depicted by Dionysius and Virgil compels me to focus briefly on the religious virtue of *pietas*. Perhaps the most familiar symbol common to Roman political and religious life was the value and role of *pietas*. Virgil records that Aeneas was chosen by the divinity for his mission and was constantly under the guidance of gods, and this element places Aeneas on par with Abraham. Like Abraham, Aeneas was placed under a divine promise, which was projected through time to include the future offspring of the Roman people. Not only was Aeneas promised divine protection, but that protection extended to all his future descendants.

Thus the motif of *pietas* had its origin in the promises of the gods and was even inscribed on the Roman shields used by Roman soldiers.[32] *Pietas* is linked to the journey motif, with which the narratives of Aeneas are imbued, with the watchful eye of the gods, and he trusted in the divinities. The Virgilian poem is perhaps meaningless without *pietas* because it was later adopted by the Roman Republic as its powerful badge of honor and identity. One area of religious and political practice in which the republic was known had to do with the value placed on *pietas*/*fides*/faith.

Pietas is a complex and fluid concept that includes such elements as dutifulness, devotion, piety, patriotism, and kindness.[33] The triumph of

Augustus saw a revival of the role and place of *pietas*: his own revival of Roman cultural mores and ethos was a monumental expression of his loyalty to the founders of Rome. The victories of Augustus were viewed as the will of a divine universe and linked to the emblem of *pietas*, which was firmly placed on the shield. Aeneas typically expressed the Roman ideal in his religious attitude, in his patriotic mission, and in his relations with his father, son, traditional *penates*, and his kinsmen. Virgil cast Aeneas as the hero and the pious, dutiful son of Anchises and Venus. In Virgil's work, *pietas* is that "quality for which he was known best and which came to overshadow all his other negative traits."[34]

Pietas is mainly piety toward one's ancestors, and from a religious point of view, it applies to the veneration of the gods and ancestors. In times of renewal and change, *pietas* is a sense of gratitude expressed in social, cultural, and religious terms. In book 1, Virgil portrays Aeneas as a figure who believes (1) that everything should be done in a dutiful manner, and (2) that his fame stretches to the heavens; yet he still must wander, unknown and destitute.[35] Certain schools of thought hold that "the trinity of Roman virtues, *virtus*, *pietas*, *fides*, signified self-discipline and strength of character, respect for the order of things, and honor, good faith—expressed in honoring and keeping of agreements."[36] The Roman Republic emphasized *fides*as trustworthiness, loyalty, and sincerity of the person or institution to which they turned, or the objective value of the promise they had received.[37]

In the program of Roman imperialism, *fides* was a word of basic inequality upon which patron-client relationships existed. The cultural, religious, and political atmospheres were saturated with words that would have been hard for Paul to ignore. The gospel of Augustus was not only inscribed in Latin on the inside of the temples but was also found in a Greek translation placed on the outside of the temple building. In this sense, it was clearly readable and understandable, and impossible for Paul to overlook.[38]

The Augustan period saw religion and state as inseparable, and *pietas* meant that one was to demonstrate devotion to the state—an idea far more complex than what we would call American patriotism. Fear of gods and ancestors not only made the Roman Empire so secure but also allowed the government to rule with a strong hand. The idea of control of all areas of life through religion was founded on the principle of political and religious dominance of the ruling class. The first duty of every citizen was to the class of which he or she was a member. In the Roman religious system, the individual was always subservient; his or her interests were inferior.[39]

No other hero or founder in Roman history was as self-sacrificing as Aeneas. He was not only a hero but also a pious founder whose personal interests were subdued by divine fate.[40] As a gesture of devotion, Augustus venerated his ancestor through engravings of the monuments and public buildings of the first and second centuries ce, which testify to the unprecedented popularity of the pious-Aeneas theme during that period.[41] Not only was Aeneas's piety commemorated on monuments, but emperors paid homage to it by placing Aeneas's likeness on coins. In the time of Augustus, the Roman Empire was saturated with images either of founding fathers or those of Augustus, especially on coins and even in public temples.[42] In the *Aeneid*, Virgil demonstrates through Aeneas that "honor was attained solely by action, not by vague aspiration, and piety was achieved by correct performance of one's religious obligations."[43]

At its deepest core, piety cautions one to respect the universal community of humankind. The gods drive Aeneas to find a city in which people of different races would reside as relatives. It is not by living as we please that we realize truth and happiness, but by listening to the calling—a calling from the deity to mortal. Only this piety, this faith within Aeneas, makes it possible for him to fulfill the divine mission.[44] Thus it seems that Roman morality had practically nothing to do with religion. In that regard, Roman religion was merely an emanation of the principle of social order and moral restraint that guided the people in their everyday lives.

Socially and religiously, Aeneas is a model of *pietas*. Throughout book 3 of the *Aeneid*, Aeneas is deeply conscious of his pastoral role to his people, and he follows heaven's will and leads people to Italy, trusting only in the divine signals. In *Aeneid* 3.493–505, the Trojan hero's deep emotion is spoken with tears when considering the voyage he and his men are to undertake. But he reiterates that he is prepared to follow the commandments of divine fate. Aeneas is not the only one singled out for his *pietas*, however, nor is any particular action associated with this concept. Rather, this characteristic is applied to all known Trojan ancestors of the Romans, and Trojan descent per se is equated with *pietas*.[45]

The next question to be investigated is how the Julian family appropriated *pietas* as an ideal Roman principle to ennoble their family. Under Augustan rule, the principle of piety acquired immense political significance. It is interesting to see how piety was used to provide a moral justification for the Roman policy of conquest and also to provide the philosophical ideological background and sanction for Augustus's principate. By "the second century ce, the Trojan genealogy had ceased being the prerogative of the imperial family and had become the common property of the entire Roman people."[46] In this period, *pietas* gained its spiritual and religious significance because Roman rulers "placed the emphasis on their spiritual inheritance from Aeneas, and Aeneas was presented as the legendary model of the emperor."[47]

To be endowed as an emperor meant that one was the ideal statesman destined to have a major role in the ideal government; he was the citizen who would compel everyone, with the force of his authority and with legal punishments, to do what the philosophers could persuade only a few individuals to do. The emperor was the man with *pietas.* Aeneas's *pietas* thus prefigures the piety of Augustus, a man destined to revive the religious worldview of the Roman people.[48] This principle was greatly promulgated among both Greeks and Romans, and as such the inhabitants prided themselves on their sense of justice and, later, on their humanity. Particularly, their conquest of other nations was to be based on *pietas*. Paul Zanker puts it well when he argues that "pietas was more than just one of the virtues of the princes recorded on the honorary shield. It was to become one of the most important leitmotifs of the Augustan era."[49] As a political and religious virtue, *pietas* was engraved on the Augustan "honorary shield," and was indeed a symbol of Roman power.[50]

After the period of Aeneas, *pietas* became the device of the new Roman state—a symbol of ideological power. *Pietas* appeared widely in literature and art, a phenomenon that clearly shows to what extent the dogma had become the common property of all the Roman elite. Virgil throughout books 1–12 of the *Aeneid* venerates the piety of Aeneas at the request of Augustus himself. It is fascinating to note how Virgil emphasizes the piety of Aeneas; he even has Aeneas say of himself, *sum pius Aeneas*("I am the pious Aeneas").[51]

Book 4 portrays the striking character of Aeneas. After yielding to his love for Dido and basking at length in the luxury the queen has offered him, Aeneas suddenly changes his mind when the goddess warns him to remember his calling and, without letting himself be moved by Dido's touching laments and pleas, rapidly prepares to leave. Depicted in this tragic conflict is a clash between self-interest and divine calling. Aeneas is a hero because he sacrifices his own desires for the formidable task of seeking a new land for the fugitives from Troy, for whom a glorious future awaits. Even Queen Dido in her unhappy state is a witness to Aeneas's piety. As she watches Aeneas sail away, she calls out, "Behold, that is the honor and faith of him of whom they say that he carries with him the home-gods of his fathers and that he took his old and decrepit father on his shoulders."[52]

Two points are crucial for this book. First, the queen bases her lament on Aeneas's piety, which she does not fully understand. Second, as she laments, she curses Aeneas and cries prophetically that an avenger of Carthaginian blood will arise to complete the deserved punishment in a bitter war against Aeneas's descendants.[53] This surely should take our attention to the war with Hannibal and the Punic Wars, which occurred as a result of Aeneas's piety. Deprived of poetic symbolism, the wars were a necessary consequence of Rome's obedience to the divine calling.

Having delineated the path that Aeneas's *pietas* took, I can conclude that the concept, which has its origin in Trojan ancestry, was appropriated by Greeks and Romans as a reconciling and collaborative tool. Aeneas, in this sense, becomes not just a hero but also a king, founder, and ancestor of both Greeks and Romans. *Pietas* is a concept inseparable from the names of Aeneas and Augustus. Paul and his audience must have known the details and meaning attached to *pietas*. In the period when Paul wrote, this concept went through rapid innovations, and Pauline exegesis must begin to take account of the conditions of the actual readers of Paul and their associations and reactions as inhabitants of the Roman Empire, and must give more consideration to the aggressive ideology of the Augustan empire. Both the *Res Gestae Divi Augusti* and the *Aeneid* are the best candidates for intertextually reading the Epistle to the Romans.

After Augustus, Emperor Tiberius made *pietas* into a goddess, but this still did not mean much to the people. Consequently, under Tiberius, the ethics of Christianity was summarized as "love of God and neighbor." Thus the ambivalence of the term *pietas* is associated with the manner in which the concept was exploited by the Julio-Claudian family in its ideological appetite for ruling other nations, tribes, and races. The essence, then, of this exploitation makes powerful ruling classes claim founding figures into cults, meant to serve their interests and the interests of those after them.

Alongside the notion of *pietas* as a Roman virtue sits the religious and most common construction of ancestor cult. It would be an oversight to assume that Aeneas was never appropriated into some kind of a cult. Indeed, the Julio-Claudian family venerated Aeneas and to an extent transformed his tradition into a cult. In erecting a temple to the divine Julius Caesar, Augustus followed the model of Aeneas, who made a sacrifice and vowed to construct a temple to his father, Anchises. In the *Aeneid*, Virgil created an imaginary temple to Augustus, who "shall possess the shrine, and he adorned it with Jove's Trojan progeny with statues that breathe of the seed of Assaracus and the great names of the race sprung from Jove."[54] Linked by kinship to the Trojan *Penates*, to Vesta, and even to Apollo, all of whom he ministered to as Pontifex Maximus, Augustus sacrificed to the ancestral cult, while as emperor he basked in the worship that devolved from these associations.[55] With the institution of ancestral cult, Augustus became both a priest and a political figure.[56] Here again religion was embedded in the political structure of the state, and consequently, ancestral cult worship developed into an official religion.[57]

The invention of the Aeneas cult can be seen in the institution of coin issues, which was central during the period of Augustus. A good example is a denarius issued during the reign of Augustus at Segesta; on each side was minted the figure of Aeneas carrying his father, Anchises.[58] Another distinctive example is a "sestertius issued during the reign of Antonius Pius."[59] The reverse shows Aeneas carrying Anchises who, *capite veleto*, holds the *cista sacra* with the *Penates* in his lap. This was the famous denarius issued by Julius Caesar in 48 bce.[60] On this coin, Aeneas does not wear armor; rather, he is portrayed in a much more vigorous and warlike manner than on the Antonian sestertius. The representation of Aeneas as a nude warrior follows the Greek tradition and is further evidence of Caesar's preference for Greek models—a preference known especially from the architecture he commissioned. This distinctive culture of the Greeks was appropriated by Augustus in his consolidation of Greeks and Romans. Again, the cult of Aeneas functions as a symbol of reconciliation between Greeks and Romans.

Interestingly, on the coin, Aeneas does not lead his son but instead carries the Palladium, which is a more martial emblem of Troy's survival than the sacred chest with the peaceful household gods. Like all the Julii, Caesar claimed to have descended from Aeneas and Venus, and his emphasizing this Trojan descent is likely the primary reason the coin was issued, especially since the head of Venus appears on the obverse.[61] Related to this issue of coins is the propagation of imperial propaganda, because "good news would be printed on the local coins."[62] A similar situation exists today, in which the whole world uses American currency in business transactions. For Augustus, the imperial cult was a way of subduing the whole world, and conquered nations served by Rome's effective techniques of mass production and standardization would pay homage to the emperor.[63]

Months in the Roman world were named after heroes and ancestors, another way in which imperial propaganda was reinforced. Although no month was named after Aeneas, Sextilis was made into August, and Quintilius made into July. The Greco-Roman world is popularly known for games, and most of these games were to honor great benefactors, sometimes kings and, occasionally, Roman commanders who had led successful war expeditions. In sum, the Aeneas cult culminated in Augustus's political administration of the empire. The offering of the cult of Caesar should be perceived as a novelty on the part of Augustus. What emerged was a complex interaction of the past and the present of which the past defined and informed the ideology of the ruling class. However, all the attendant rituals and beliefs that were developed along traditional lines led to the worship of the imperial family—Augustus himself became a living Roman ancestor. In sum, all was due to Augustus's power in reforming and bringing Rome to its golden age.

Therefore, the central importance of ancestral practice in the Augustan ideology was stamped with a religion. The cult of Aeneas is an invention of shared history being exploited into a myth of origin in defining a sense of cultural and ethnic identity. Thus what Paul wrote in Romans is a response to a culture that was deeply oriented toward the preservation of the past upon which the continuity of Roman ideology was firmly anchored. It is a story of self-definition, identity, and elevation. It is a story of founding ancestors, which is also at the root of Paul's Letter to the Romans. The public lauded Augustus as the iconic figure of imperial virtue, and he was celebrated in the *forum Augustum* as the culmination of Aeneas's fate-ordained history. Augustus became the new Aeneas destined to exercise imperial rule throughout the world. Dieter Georgi has noted that "the gospel according to Augustus had the world spellbound,"[64] including, presumably, some of the Roman Christians to whom Paul later wrote. Paradoxically, New Testament scholars remain politically conservative as to the context in which Paul wrote Romans.

This chapter has pursued the fundamental shift in the location of power, especially during the Augustan era. This period was not only revolutionary but also formed on self-evaluation, identity formation, and renewal of genealogical ties from the ancient foundations of the Roman Empire. Through the writings of Dionysius and Virgil, the empire emerged as an elite group and demonstrated its power by control of knowledge of the past. In all respects, the Augustan revolution was indeed oriented toward a revolution of power, identity, and knowledge. Without Aeneas, the imperial propaganda of Augustus would have lost its power. In Dionysius and Virgil, the Trojan connection helped to create a powerful pedigree for the Julian family and, consequently, for all the successors of Augustus. Political and cultural motives combined to develop a narrative that would bring mutual esteem to Romans and Latins and establish a pedigree that connected Rome to the Hellenic world.[65] The writers and historians of the Augustan age reshaped the narrative for the needs of their time to effect reconciliation and friendship between Greeks and Trojans.

The cult of Aeneas, which Augustus transformed into an emperor cult, helped Paul to creatively advance his gospel using the language and culture of the day. The terminological and conceptual overlaps between the imperial and Pauline gospels ensured that elements of Paul's message would have attracted or repulsed Greeks and Romans. What emerged can only be described as a scandal for all cultures in the Hellenistic world because Paul's construction of Abraham as a spiritual ancestor greatly surpassed Aeneas and other related Greco-Roman ancestors. Thus chapter 5 will offer a brief comparison of Aeneas and Abraham; consequently, it will offer a theological understanding of ways through which Paul's Abraham can be contextualized in other cultures of the world.

Notes

1. 1 Cor. 1:18-31. See Also Erich Gruen, "The Making of the Trojan Legend," in *Culture and National Identity in Republican Rome* (Ithaca: Cornell University Press, 1992), 29–41.

2. See chapter 3 of this book.

3. The program of cultural and religious revival is well illustrated in Paul Zanker, *The Power of Images in the Age of Augustus* (Ann Arbor: University of Michigan Press, 1990), 101–2.

4. See Brigitte Kahl, *Galatians Re-Imagined: Reading with the Eyes of the Vanquished* (Minneapolis: Fortress Press, 2010), 281–89.

5. Israel Kamudzandu, *Abraham as Spiritual Ancestor: A Postcolonial Zimbabwe Reading of Romans 4* (Leiden: Brill, 2010), 47.

6. Acts 17:16-34 has Paul watching and listening to the Athenians worshiping and celebrating their religion, a situation he utilizes to spiritually construct a theology of ancestry based on Abraham.

7. Marianne Palmer Bonz, *The Past as Legacy: Luke-Acts and Ancient Epic* (Minneapolis: Fortress Press, 2000).

8. Virgil, *Aeneid* 1.1–7.

9. Gruen, *Culture and National Identity*, 6–51.

10. Virgil, *Aeneid* 1.1-5. Here Aeneas is hailed as a hero who sailed from Troy and wandered to Italy with a command from the gods to build a capital of the nations.

11. See Arnold Momigliano, "How to Reconcile Greeks and Trojans," in *On Pagans, Jews and Christians* (Middletown, CT: Wesleyan University Press, 1987), 264–85.

12. J. Bremmer and N. M. Horshfall, *Roman Myth and Mythography* (London: University of London, 1987), 13.

13. See Momigliano, "How to Reconcile Greeks and Trojans," 273.

14. See P. A. Brunt and J. M. Moore, eds., *Res Gestae Divi Augusti: The Achievements of the Divine Augustus* (Oxford: Oxford University Press, 1967), 3–7.

15. Ibid., 29.

16. *Aeneid* 1.1–7.

17. Translation from *The Internet Classic Archive*, "The Aeneid by Virgil," trans. John Dryden, http://classics.mit.edu/Virgil/aeneid.1.i.html

18. Zanker, *The Power of Images*, 104–5.

19. Ibid., 101.

20. Momigliano, *On Pagans*, 274.

21. G. Karl Galinsky, *Aeneas, Sicily, and Rome* (Princeton: Princeton University Press, 1969), 103–41.

22. Dionysius of Halicarnassus, *Antiquitates romanae* 1.61.

23. Zanker, *The Power of Images*, 102.

24. Andrew Wallace-Hadrill, *Rome's Cultural Revolution* (Cambridge: Cambridge University Press, 2008), 233.

25. Ibid., 229.

26. Ibid., 148.

27. Dionysius of Halicarnassus, *Antiquitates romanae* 1.59.1–2

28. Dionysius of Halicarnassus, *Antiquitates romanae* 1.64.4–5, 1.65.1–2, and 1.66.1–5.

29. Dionysius of Halicarnassus, *Antiquitates romanae* 1.68.4

30. See Wallace-Hadrill, *Rome's Cultural Revolution*, 226–27.

31. See Livy, *Ab Urbe Condita libri* 1.2.6; See also Virgil, *Aeneid* 12.794–95.

32. Zanker, *The Power of Images*, 103.

33. D. P. Simpson, *Casell's Compact Latin Dictionary* (New York: Dell, 1963), 169. See also H. Wagenvoort, "Pietas," in *Studies in Greek and Roman Religion*, ed. H. S. Versnell (Leiden: Brill, 1980), 1:7

34. Galinsky, *Aeneas, Sicily, and Rome*, 4. This book contains a chapter on Pius Aeneas.

35. Virgil, *Aeneid* 1.378–79, 384.

36. D. M. Field, *Greek and Roman Mythology* (New York: Chartwell, 1977), 179. See also Momigliano, *On Pagans*; in the chapter titled "Religion in Athens, Rome, and Jerusalem," he states that "fides meant the restoration of commercial credit, or as an emotional bond between the living and the dead: perhaps less so between man and gods," 76–77.

37. Momigliano, *On Pagans*, 77–78.

38. See Brunt and Moore, *Res Gestae Divi Augusti*, 1–7.

39. Ibid.

40. Ibid.

41. See Galinsky, *Aeneas, Sicily, and Rome*, 5, who argues that Julius Caesar issued a famous denarius in 48 BCE, on which Aeneas is portrayed in a much more vigorous and warlike manner than on the Antonine sestertius.

42. Zanker, *The Power of Images*, 104–35.

43. Field, *Greek and Roman Mythology*, 179.

44. This notion is clearly stated in Homer's *Iliad* (20.307), where Poseidon prophesies that Aeneas and his descendants will rule over the Trojans. In other books of the *Iliad*, Aeneas fights against the Greeks, exhibits marked piety toward gods (20.347), and is himself honored like a god (11.58). Out of this tradition developed the legend of Aeneas's flight from Troy. By Virgil's time, Aeneas's founding of Rome had become a national legend.

45. This synthesis is given poignancy by Galinsky, *Aeneas, Sicily, and Rome*, which contains a chapter on Pius Aeneas.

46. Galinsky, *Aeneas, Sicily, and Rome*, 6.

47. Ibid.

48. Zanker, *The Power of Images*, 102.

49. Ibid., 102–3.

50. Ibid.

51. Virgil, *Aeneid* 1.378.

52. Virgil, *Aeneid* 4.597–600.

53. Virgil, *Aeneid* 4.625–70. This part of the poem presents a prophetic curse, foretelling that Aeneas's descendants will have to fight wars as a result of his abandonment of Queen Dido.

54. Virgil, *Aeneid* 5.62.

55. Marie Tanner, *The Last Descendant of Aeneas: The Hapsburgs and the Mythic Image of the Emperor* (New Haven: Yale University Press, 1993), 68.

56. Wallace-Hadrill, *Rome's Cultural Revolution*, 249

57. See Peter Garnsey and Richard Saller, eds., *The Roman Empire: Economy, Society and Culture* (Berkeley: University of California Press, 1987), 163–77.

58. Andrew Burnett, Michel Amandry, and Pere Pau Ripolles, eds., *Roman Provincial Coinage: From the Death of Caesar to the Death of Vitellius (44BC–AD 69)* (London: British Museum Press, 1992), 1:173. See also vol. 2, plates 652 and 2306, where Aeneas has his father on his shoulders.

59. Galinsky, *Aeneas, Sicily, and Rome*, 4–5.

60. Ibid., 5.

61. Ibid.

62. Ramsay MacMullen, *Romanization in the Time of Augustus* (New Haven: Yale University Press, 2000), 14.

63. On coinage in Rome, see Wallace-Hadrill, *Rome's Cultural Revolution*, 224.

64. Dieter Georgi, "Who Is the True Prophet?" *Harvard Theological Review* 79 (1986): 1–3. See also Ben Witherington III, *Conflict and Community in Corinth: A Socio-Rhetorical Commentary on 1 and 2 Corinthians* (Grand Rapids: Eerdmans, 1995), 295–98.

65. Gruen, "Making of Trojan Legend," 50.

5

Aeneas and Abraham Paradigms

Throughout this book I have argued that ancestral practices—*mores maiorum*—are important signatures upon which cultures of the world seek to preserve the traditions of the past and use them to inform and guide both the present and the future. I have argued that Paul, as well as his communities of Jews, Greeks, and Romans, were aware of ancestor traditions, especially the Augustan allegiance to founding figures. I have argued and will continue to emphasize that Pauline exegesis must begin to take into account the conditions of people's context when reading biblical texts.

Paul's Letter to the Romans cannot be understood without taking into perspective the Augustan construction of the Aeneas legend, which acquired a canonical character and functioned as the official ideology of the Roman state. For the Julio-Claudian religion, the *Aeneid* became, in relation to the Homeric epics, something like the New Testament in relation to the Old Testament of the Judeo-Christian Bible. And in the end, the *Aeneid* finally replaced the epic of Homer as the bible of Hellenism. Thematically and in story form, Genesis 12–22 and the *Aeneid* are strikingly similar in tone and style. And that in itself is the crux of this project, a similarity that, as I have discovered in retrospect, also parallels what happened in Africa during and after the colonial period (1890–1980).[1]

On both a political and a religious level, Paul reconstructed Abraham as a spiritual ancestor of all who imitate his faith and thus invited less privileged cultures to locate their faith in this less privileged human figure. The aim of this chapter is to articulate a contextualized theology of Paul and to reassert my contention that the possibilities and potentials of contextualizing Paul and Abraham in a postcolonial African context are endless. In the previous chapter, I outlined the process through which the works of Dionysius of Halicarnassus and Virgil reconstituted the importance of Roman ideology based on ancestral practices. Since much has been written about Abraham, the following will be a brief analysis of the works of two Hellenistic-Jewish historians: namely, the Hellenistic Jewish philosopher Philo (20 BCE–50 CE), and the Romano-Jewish historian and hagiographer Flavius Josephus (37 CE–C. 100 CE), who wrote about the ancestral greatness of Abraham and fashioned his image in a way similar to Virgil and Dionysius's reconstruction of Aeneas. The analysis is meant to expose the typological, political, religious, and social possibilities in both Aeneas and Abraham and to use the paradigm in the exegesis of Paul's theology of Abraham. The poignancy of this analysis will lead into a theological appreciation of Paul and ancestors in postcolonial Africa.

Abraham in Philo

The Abraham's ancestry was great not only according to the Jewish worldview but also, as developed by Philo and Josephus, in the Hellenistic-Jewish world of Greeks and Romans.[2] The narrative of Abraham in both Philo and Josephus exposes complex and manifold personalities and ancestral virtues. Hellenistic Jewish authors sought to elevate the image of Abraham beyond that of Roman ancestors. Abraham is portrayed as a model of piety whose allegiance was only to God and as a statesman whose virtues encompassed those of both Greek and Roman philosophers. Philo ascribes to Abraham what he calls "virtues."[3] These virtues represent Jewish ideals as told through Stoic and Platonic concepts, and are similar to those ascribed to Greek and Roman ancestors.

Philo develops his allegorical account of Abraham's neotic progress by following the stages of the Genesis narrative. Philo's Abraham is a wise man made perfect through teachings of the law.[4] In this sense, Philo uses the story of Abraham to address the virtue of knowledge and thus assists both Greeks and Romans to appreciate their Jewish ancestors/founders. Typologically, Philo portrays Abraham's experience as a progression in knowledge by which Abraham moves through definite stages of intelligence.[5] Philo asserts that Abraham's wandering from Chaldea to Haran allegorically meant that Abraham advanced from material to spiritual knowledge (*Migr.* 192).

Philo associates Abraham's advance in reason with the change of Abraham's name, stating that Abraham's new name means "elect father of sound" or "uplifted father."[6] Here Abraham is transformed into a higher figure who surpasses even Greek and Roman heroes. Philo also charts Abraham's progress toward knowledge by analyzing his relationship with Hagar and his vision of the three angels at Mamre (Genesis 18). Related to this is also the notion of Abraham as a wise philosopher. In Philo, Abraham is the ideal wise man, who first searched for God, thus elevating the ancestor from a purely nationalistic figure to a more diverse person—one who can be appropriated by other cultures. He is not only a wise man but also a world citizen (*Migr.* 59) and a philosopher-king (*Abr.* 261; *Mut.* 151–53; *De Somniis* 2.244).[7] In Philo, Abraham emerges as a Middle Platonist sage similar to Greek and Roman philosophers.[8] This creative approach by Philo appealed not only to the Jews in the Hellenistic world but to all Hellenes who were well acquainted with the traditions of great founders.

Abraham, the ancestor of Jews and the transmitter of culture to other people, appears in Philo with the virtue of piety. Philo views piety as the greatest virtue, one that makes Jewish culture superior to other cultures (*Abr.* 60–61). Abraham was not alone in possessing such qualities: figures such as Moses, Daniel, Esther, Enoch, Noah, Isaac, Sarah, Jacob, and Cain held great attraction for the Jewish people (Heb. 11:1-40). Abraham's piety includes his love for and obedience toward God (*Abr.* 170, 192). This piety is further demonstrated in his willingness to sacrifice Isaac (*Abr.* 167–207), his prayer for God's intervention against Pharaoh (*Abr.* 93–98), and his hospitality toward the angelic visitors (*Abr.* 114–16).[9] Philo views piety and faith as two complementary virtues found in Abraham, and thus he describes the ancestor in Hellenic fashion and, for a Hellenistic readership, an attractive ancestor. Drawing from the Septuagint, Philo defines faith (πίστις/*pistis*) as trusting in God's future provision as if it were already a reality. In *Migr.* 44, we find the following:

> ἀρτηθεῖσα γὰρ καὶ ἐκκρεμασθεῖσα ἐλπίδος χρηστῆς καὶ ἀνενδοίαστα νομίσασα ἤδη παρεῖναι τὰ μὴ παρόντα διὰ τὴν τοῦ ὑποσχομένου βεβαιότητα πίστιν, ἀγαθὸν τέλειον, ἆθλον εὕρηται· καὶ γὰρ αὖθις λέγεται, ὅτι "ἐπίστευσεν Ἀβραὰμ τῷ θεῷ
>
> For the soul, clinging in utter dependence on a good hope and deeming that things not present are beyond question already present by reason of the sure steadfastness of Him that promised them, has won as its meed faith, a perfect good; for we read a little later "Abraham believed God."[10]

Thus faith means a hope that clings to God's faithfulness. In further elaboration, Philo argues that "faith in God is the one safe and infallible good. It is the consolation of life, the fulfillment of bright hopes, the death of ills, the harvest of goods, the acquaintance with piety, and the heritage of happiness. It is the all-round betterment of the soul firmly fastened on God."[11]

The meaning and manifestation of faith in Hebrew culture is drawn from Abraham's experiences during his call from the land of Chaldea. In another version, called the *Quis Rerum Divinarum Heres.* 90–93, Philo describes Abraham's faith as being "unalloyed trust" in God. In this case, he defines faith as utter dependence on God, as trusting God without any reliance on the material order. This is similar to Paul's articulation of Abraham's faith in Rom. 4:19. Here the object of faith is God, and in Rom. 4:19, Abraham's faith in God, who surmounts the physical death of his body and that of Sarah, would indeed appeal to all nations (Gen. 17:4-6). The Israelite ancestor modeled faith not only in abstract terms but also by believing in the promises of God, and consequently modeling for Christian believers' faith in the resurrection of Jesus. Equally significant, Philo's Abraham eclipses Greek and Roman gods and locates the Jewish patriarch at the center of diverse cultures, thus modeling Abraham into a malleable figure.

In the Septuagint, Gen. 24:1, Abraham is the first to be called an elder, a quality Philo creatively uses to elevate Abraham above and beyond all Greco-Roman ancestors. Philo presents Abraham as the first person who surpassed all humans in divine endowments and in achievements, and his capacities brought benefits to the universe.[12] In essence, the Abraham encountered in Philo was the first to possess faith. Faith makes Abraham the harbinger of God's ethnos. Thus God holds Abraham's faith in high esteem and repays this faith with divine faith; God confirms by an oath the gifts already promised. God's oath is a measure of faith added to that faith Abraham antecedently possessed.[13]

The prominence of Abraham's faith is seen in the way God called, guided, and transformed the life of Abraham and Sarah, as well as their descendants.[14] Astounded by Abraham's faith, God addresses him as a friend would address an acquaintance (*Abr.* 273). In a striking manner, God converses with Abraham in fictive-kinship terms; God's promises are met with Abraham's faith or trust. Thus, when humanity encounters God's promises, they should trust in them most firmly. The first of this human race was Abraham, the one who deserves to be the harbinger of a new humanity. Moses obeyed the law, but Abraham was the embodiment of the law, and his character and actions have "a leitmotif for Jewish pride in ancestral achievements that extended to the enhancement or even generation of foreign cultures."[15]

In *Abr.* 268, Philo defines faith as a work that results from God's providential protection and prosperity. Thus Abraham exhibited this greatest virtue: "The greatness of faith is to be found in its subject as well as its object."[16] The prominence given to Abraham by Philo indicates the extent to which Jewish authors were involved in an apologetic ancestral tradition associated with founding fathers. Faith encompasses a radical trust in God, belief in God's existence, and attainment of a blessed life. Not only that, but Philo also views Abraham as the ideal proselyte,[17] because he was the first to have faith in God (*De Virtutibus* 211–15). In the words of Francis Watson, "The classic instance of Abraham's heroic and unwavering trust in the invisible and distrust for the visible is to be found in his offering of his son in obedience to the divine command, after which the promise was confirmed by a divine oath because God himself marveled at Abraham's faith in him"[18] (*Virt.* 273).

Philo sums up the lifestyle of Abraham before God in the following: "Abraham believed in God." This was emphasized in Paul's expression of Abraham's belief that Sarah would become pregnant and that out of her dead womb God would bring forth new life, and those who imitate the faith of Israel's ancestor would also receive the same promise (Rom. 4:18-19; 5:2-5; 8:24-25). God was the object of Abraham's constant trust, thus making Paul's Abraham a model of loyal and obedient faith. Abraham became the recipient of God's promises, the beneficiary of the future divine saving action of which he was promised, because that promise was divinely ordained of God and therefore credible and irrevocable. In fact, this aspect of faith was the one counted as righteousness (Rom. 4:22). Thus the divine promise insistently shaped and molded his life by setting it in the light of the world's eschatological future. Abraham's response to the promise was a model to his followers. Isaac, the seed of the promise, would also include all future faith generations—those who will be heirs to Jesus Christ (Rom. 5:17). Those who have faith, like Abraham did, will also qualify to be spiritual heirs. Thus Philo and Paul both portray Abraham as the model of faith par excellence; Paul even calls him the "ancestor of all who have faith" in God (Rom. 4:11–12).

Related to faith are virtues of ethics and the courage that Abraham exhibited as a Jewish hero. Philo describes Abraham's ethical practice in terms of the Stoic cardinal virtues of justice, bravery, prudence, and temperance.[19] He finds these virtues in the accounts of Abraham's separation from Lot (*Abr.* 208–24), Abraham's victory over the kings (*Abr.* 225–44), and Abraham's acceptance of Sarah's death without grief (*Abr.* 245, 255–61). Philo interprets Abraham's victory over the kings as an allegory, indicating that Abraham conquered all of his physical passions.

In Philo, Abraham's virtues embody the entire Torah. In this sense, Philo's emphasis on Abraham's virtue is an emphasis on Abraham's lawful character. Writing for both Jewish and Hellenistic audiences, Philo believes that stories about the patriarchs are meant to encourage adherence to the law. This is probable because Philo is appealing to the Romans and the Alexandrians to accept the validity of Judaism as a religious/philosophical system, at a time when Jewish rights were under strain.[20] He does so by representing the law in terms of the Stoic law of nature and of Platonic idealism. [21] As an emblematic hero of the past, Abraham would be a model for all peoples, nations, and races and, ultimately, embrace the ancestors of Hellas's founding figures. Thus Philo presents Abraham as one who kept the unwritten law of nature. Because the ideal law is an archetype of the Sinaitic law, Abraham's actions serve as a model, calling the ethnos to emulate the founding ancestor. In eulogizing and praising the Jewish founders, Philo wrote the following:

> οὗτοι δέ εἰσιν ἀνδρῶν οἱ ἀνεπιλήπτως καὶ καλῶς βιώσαντες, ὧν τὰς ἀρετὰς ἐν ταῖς ἱερωτάταις ἐστηλιτεῦσθαι γραφαῖς συμβέβηκεν, οὐ πρὸς τὸν ἐκείνων ἔπαινον αὐτὸ μόνον, ἀλλὰ καὶ ὑπὲρ τοῦ τοὺς ἐντυγχάνοντας προτρέψασθαι καὶ ἐπὶ τὸν ὅμοιον ζῆλον ἀγαγεῖν. οἱ γὰρ ἔμψυχοι καὶ λογικοὶ νόμοι ἄνδρες ἐκεῖνοι γεγόνασιν, οὓς δυοῖν χάριν ἐσέμνυνεν·
>
> These are such men as lived good and blameless lives, whose virtues stand permanently recorded in the most holy scriptures, not merely to sound their praises but for the instruction of the reader and as an inducement to him to aspire to the same; for in these men we have laws endowed with life and reason[22]

The principal reason Philo presents Abraham is to encourage Jews to emulate their founder both in conduct and in faith. In *Abr.* 5, Philo states that the stories of the patriarchs were included in the Pentateuch to show that the law is consistent with nature and that it is not too difficult to keep.

Philo also views Abraham through a "Hellenistic garb for a judiciously selected apologetic occasion."[23] This double presentation serves both of Philo's audiences, namely, Greco-Romans and Hellenistic Jews. In the apologetic sense, Abraham is transformed from a sage into a faith figure, one who is in full possession of his faith. His faith or trust in God is the mark of his piety and firmly roots him in God.

While Abraham possessed the virtue of faith, we also discover that, as a friend of God, he received the gift of wisdom—a quality Philo appropriated from Greek and Roman philosophy to elevate Abraham above Roman emperors and heroes. Thus Abraham shared some of this multifaceted prowess with other Greek sages but surpassed them in religious values and ideals. In Samuel Sandmel's words, "Abraham, as a prophet and friend of God, passes beyond the bounds of human happiness. He becomes nobly born, registering God as his father and becoming by adoption His only son, and thus achieves divine wisdom."[24]

In other words, Abraham apprehended the *sophia*of God. When Abraham's soul encountered God's presence, God did not turn away but in love of this virtue-loving soul, God came forward to meet with him. This is what God saw in Abraham and reckoned to him as righteousness (Gen. 15:6; cf. Rom. 4:3). Philo portrays Abraham as the beneficiary of God's power, thus making him the ancestor of all people, "no matter which cultural and theological tendency they represent."[25] Similarly, in *4 Maccabees* Abraham is again portrayed as a model of piety. His descendants are supposed to be the ideal Jews who practice piety toward the law. In *4 Macc.*9:22, the term "son of Abraham" refers to one who exhibits piety toward the law.[26] In most cases, the term "son of Abraham" would draw attention to Abraham's character as the model for piety. However, in *4 Maccabees* the model is not Abraham, but Isaac, who allowed himself to be offered as a sacrifice for the sake of piety (*4 Macc.* 13:12, 18:11).[27] Isaac is commended for offering himself as a true "son of Abraham, who uttered not a groan" (*4 Macc.* 9: 21; cf. 16:20). As the son of promise, Isaac instructed his brothers to imitate his actions and die for the sake of their religion (*4 Macc.* 9:23). In this case, both Abraham and Isaac are examples of true piety. The piety of the founding ancestor is reflected in Isaac, the ideal son, and in descendants who will imitate Isaac.

Abraham in Josephus

Like Philo, Josephus chooses aspects of Abraham's story that fit his agenda and portrays Abraham with many Greco-Roman motifs. His first move minimizes the role of the covenant in order to deemphasize Jewish particularism before his Roman audience.[28] Certain sections of the Genesis portrayals of Abraham are omitted. Josephus separates Abraham from the law most likely in order to appeal to the Romans to accept Judaism culturally and politically, while not requiring them to practice the religion. Thus, in order to fit his apologetic and propagandistic aims, Josephus picks and chooses which aspects of Abraham to emphasize.[29]

Like other Jewish writers in Diaspora, Josephus wants to make Judaism acceptable to both Greeks and Romans. To accomplish this, Josephus portrays Abraham as a Greek philosopher and military leader.[30] In *Jewish Antiquities*1.154, Josephus describes Abraham as a philosopher who made inferences and participated in philosophical debates. Not only that, but Abraham was the first to arrive at monotheism, an aspect that would have appealed to most Hellenes. In Josephus's portrayal, "the patriarch emerges as the typical national hero, such as was popular in Hellenistic times, with emphasis on his noble genealogy, his qualities as a convincing speaker, a logician, a philosopher, a scientist, a general, and the supremely good host to strangers."[31]

Josephus's attribution to Abraham of military characteristics would also have been impressive to his Greco-Roman audience. In *Ant.* 1.159–60, Josephus includes a tradition from Nicolas of Damascus, which states that Abraham invaded Damascus with a large army. The tradition also states that Abraham reigned for some time as a king in Damascus. Not only does Josephus take this from other historians, but he also includes his own portrayal of Abraham's military leadership by inserting military terminology into the account of Abraham's victory over kings (*Ant.* 1.181–82; Gen. 14:1-24).

Writing for the Roman audience, Josephus paints Abraham as a model of divine providence, asserting that even though Abraham had a boundless army, he trusted instead in divine providence. Abraham's trust in this providence resulted in his prosperity and Sarah's protection; a version that is absent in Philo. With regard to his treatment of Abraham's wars with the kings (*Ant.* 1.171–82), Josephus speaks against relying on arms rather than God. For Josephus, the account indicates that "victory does not depend on numbers and a multitude of hands" (*Ant.* 1.178), but on God, who delivered Abraham's enemies into his hands (*Ant.* 1.181). Josephus also describes the sacrifice of Isaac as an event that displayed divine providence, with God as the divine assistant (*Ant.* 1.222–36). Josephus explains Abraham's willingness to make the sacrifice as trust in divine providence: "That in everything he must submit to His will, since all that befell His favored ones was ordained by his providence" *(Ant.* 1.125). Josephus adds a speech by Abraham in which he tells Isaac to trust in God's will, since God is his "supporter and ally" (*Ant.* 1.229). In this case, Josephus portrays God as the intermediary who intercedes for Abraham in times of need, an aspect that would indeed have appealed to Greeks and Romans, especially those who participated in ancestral cults.

In both Philo and Josephus, the notion of monotheism is clearly spelled out but with different emphases. In Josephus, it is Abraham's intelligence, persuasiveness, and philosophical ability that set the stage for his recognition of one God. Here Josephus makes use of that which the Greeks and Romans valued, namely, the notion of being the "first."[32] Josephus creatively describes the genesis of Abraham's faith in the one God in consonance with his invention of monotheism. The way Abraham arrives at this historical discovery deserves comment as it illuminates Josephus's establishment of Abraham within the Hellenistic cultural context.

In *Ant.* 1.155–56, Josephus writes:

> διὰ τοῦτο καὶ φρονεῖν μεῖζον ἐπ' ἀρετῇ τῶν ἄλλων ἠργμένος καὶ τὴν περὶ τοῦ θεοῦ δόξαν ἣν ἅπασι συνέβαινεν εἶναι καινίσαι καὶ μεταβαλεῖν ἔγνω πρῶτος οὖν τολμᾷ θεὸνἀποφήνασθαι δημιουργὸν τῶν ὅλων ἕνα τῶν δὲ λοιπῶν εἰ καί τι πρὸς εὐδαιμονίαν συντελεῖ κατὰ προσταγὴν τὴν τούτου παρέχειν ἕκαστον καὶ οὐ κατ' οἰκείαν ἰσχύν εἰκάζεται δὲ ταῦτα τοῖς γῆς καὶ θαλάσσης παθήμασι τοῖς τε περὶ τὸν ἥλιον καὶ τὴν σελήνην καὶ πᾶσι τοῖς κατ' οὐρανὸν συμβαίνουσι δυνάμεως γὰρ αὐτοῖς παρούσης καὶ προνοῆσαι τῆς κατ' αὐτοὺς εὐταξίας ταύτης δ' ὑστεροῦντας φανεροὺς γίνεσθαι μηδ' ὅσα πρὸς τὸ χρησιμώτερον ἡμῖν συνεργοῦσι κατὰ τὴν αὐτῶν ἐξουσίαν ἀλλὰ κατὰ τὴν τοῦ κελεύοντος ἰσχὺν ὑπουργεῖν ᾧ καλῶς ἔχει μόνῳ τὴν τιμὴν καὶ τὴν εὐχαριστίαν ἀπονέμειν
>
> This he [Abraham] inferred from the changes to which land and sea are subject, from the course of sun and the moon, and from all the celestial phenomena; for he argued, were these bodies endowed with power, they would have provided for their own regularity; but, since they lacked this last, it was manifest that even those services in which they cooperate for our greater benefit they render not in virtue of their own authority, but through the might of their commanding sovereign, to whom alone it is right to render our homage and thanksgiving.[33]

In this tractate, Abraham is portrayed as a wise man and philosopher—the two virtues valued greatly by both Greeks and Romans of the Augustan period. Josephus uses Gen. 12:10-20 to propose that Abraham invented astronomy and arithmetic for the Egyptians and, consequently, for the Greeks. Josephus creatively exploits the narrative gaps in the Genesis account of Abraham's travels in order to contextualize the hero's philosophical prowess, his religious genius, and his status as a cultural hero active on the international stage. In all these portrayals, Josephus uses Abraham to define Judaism vis-à-vis Greco-Roman heroes and founders.

In Greco-Roman antiquity, the stories of wandering philosophers were common, and Josephus portrays the journeys of Abraham in the same manner. The same pattern is evident in the history of Judaism: tithing moments were to be punctuated with a narration of wandering ancestors (Deut. 26:3-5). The ancestry had reference to Abraham, who is the ancestor of the Jews (Gen. 11:31; 12:1-9; 20:13). In keeping with the Hellenistic genre of journey, Josephus makes Abraham's journey to Egypt not so much as motivated by famine as by a search for truth, just as philosophers did during that period. As Feldman rightly stresses, Josephus paints Abraham in terms that evoke Greco-Roman ideals of philosophy and wisdom, as exemplified by such figures as Solon.[34] I assert that Abraham's journey to Egypt should be seen not as a desperate move; rather, it was in alignment with the motif of wandering (Gen. 12:1-3). Like Aeneas, Abraham is a model of someone who is driven by fate to a place where he will form a new people.[35]

The fact that Josephus depicts Abraham as willing to convert if he was defeated in an argument[36]meant that he was open to others. In Josephus's portrayal of Abraham in the Egyptian saga, the hero strikingly emerges as someone worth the admiration of Greeks and Romans. Abraham is a persuasive philosopher and a passionate listener. His willingness to engage his God with the gods of other cultures makes Abraham transcend celebrated Hellenistic philosophers. Josephus devotes an entire tractate in praise of Abraham as a convincing teacher who was able to persuade his hearers on any subject.[37]

The adventures of Aeneas are sandwiched between gods who are in charge of his travels, and his future has already been determined by divine fate.[38] Aeneas embarks on an unknown journey, and the will of the gods is followed at every step until he reaches the shores of Italy (*Aeneid* 2.293–97). Similarly, Abraham's life is wholly dependent on power from God. It is God who exercises providence, which, in this case, is understood as "watchful, concerned forethought and consideration: Abraham agreed to sacrifice his son because of his belief that whatever came the way of those favored by God came through his providence."[39] The theme that providence and fate ruled the world was a popular concept in the Greco-Roman worldview. The Augustan age was imbued with the idea that the world was ruled by providence. Stoics believed that the world was "the planned and providential work of God, that human reason if correct must think in the same way as the divine reason, and that man should therefore accept willingly all that happens."[40] Piety/faith was the proper response toward the providential work of the gods. Thus Abraham was a fitting figure of piety because, when he was willing to sacrifice his son, he was aligning his mind with the mind of the divine.

Virgil's narration of Aeneas's journey resembles similar elements of the burden of fate in an ancestor's life. I argue that Josephus's employment of Greco-Roman ideals was meant to paint Abraham as the progenitor of a special people— an element that would convince Romans to regard Jews as a superior nation. Abraham discovered monotheism, a new way of relating to God, and he discovered astronomy. Above all, he was found to be virtuous in all things, a well-respected quality in the Hellenistic world. Judaism according to Josephus emerges as a superior culture with a religion that is of a far higher quality than that of the Greeks and Romans. Finally, both Philo and Josephus had apologetic concerns, and the way they wrote about Abraham was indeed a response to the ideological ancestral claim of the period. They also wrote in defense of the Jewish culture's founding fathers—a defense that was too well-entrenched to be discarded while in a foreign land. The picture emerges of Abraham as a pious figure, whose piety/faith is different from that of the Greco-Roman ancestors. Through Philo and Josephus's writings, the Jews were able to anchor themselves as a distinctive people, and such figures as Abraham, Joseph, Jacob, and Sarah gave them such audacity.

Thus a shared history or narrative of origin is a foil that protects people's sense of identity. Ancestors are therefore invoked in seasons when identity is under attack, and to invoke one's ancestor is a cry for legitimacy. In the Epistle to the Romans, Paul appeals to a stable spiritual ancestor who can be appropriated by diverse global cultures. The question that remains has to do with ways through which New Testament biblical interpreters can employ the Aeneas-Abraham paradigm to illuminate a theological exegesis of Paul in cultures where ancestry is an issue of life and death.

Notes

1. See chapters 1 and 2 of this book, where I have elaborated the encounter of the Western colonial-missionary culture with African traditional religion(s).

2. See Louis H. Feldman, *Judaism and Hellenism Reconsidered* (Leiden: Brill: 2006), 261–79.

3. Philo's ideas were greatly influenced by his allegiance to Platonism and the particular worldview with which he was in dialogue. For an elaboration of this, see Robert M. Berchman, *From Philo to Middle Platonism in Transition* (Chico, CA: Scholars, 1984), 9–20. See also John M. Dillon, *The Middle Platonists 80 B.C. to A.D. 220* (Ithaca, NY: Cornell University Press, 1977), 149–51.

4. Philo, *On Abraham* 1.68 (hereafter *Abr.*).

5. Philo, *Abr.* 57–58, 70; Philo, *Migration of Abraham* 13 and 194–96 (hereafter *Migr.*). Philo describes knowledge as a self-awakening experience by which one enters a new state of insight.

6. *Abr.* 81–84; Philo, *De mutatione nominum* 69–76 (hereafter *Mut.*).

7. Samuel Sandmel, *Philo of Alexandria. An Introduction* (Oxford: Oxford University Press, 1979), 57. A philosopher-king's laws are an extension of nature. As a divine entity,the king possesses knowledge of the divine will of nature.

8. For a discussion of Platonism, see John Dillon, *The Middle Platonists* (Ithaca, NY: Cornell University Press, 1977), 135–39. Dillon argues that Philo is the chief representative of Middle Platonism.

9. For an elaboration of this virtue, see J. T. A. G. M. Van Ruitten, "Abraham, Job and the Book of Jubilees," in *The Sacrifice of Isaac: The Aqedah (Genesis 22) and Its Interpretations*, ed. Eibert Tigchelar and Ed Noort (Leiden: Brill, 2002), 62.

10. Philo, *Migr.* 44.

11. Philo, *Abr.* 267.

12. Samuel Sandmel, *Philo of Alexandria: An Introduction* (Oxford: Oxford University Press, 1979), 140.

13. Ibid., 140.

14. Justin, *Dialogus cum Tryphone* (hereafter Justin, *Dial.*). Trypho identifies himself as a descendant of Abraham in *Dial.* 44. Justin's apologetic is reminiscent of Paul, as he attempts to convince Trypho to reject circumcision and the law.

15. Erich S. Gruen, *Heritage and Hellenism: The Reinvention of Jewish Tradition* (Berkeley: University of California Press, 1998), 146.

16. *Abr.* 269–80.

17. Karl Georg Kuhn, "προσήλυτος," in *Theological Dictionary of the New Testament*, ed. Gerhard Kittel and Gerhard Friedrich, trans. Geoffrey W. Bromiley (Grand Rapids: Eerdmans, 1968), 6:727–31, 739. In this work, "proselyte" is defined as a new creature whose former pagan life no longer exists, and he will not be punished for transgressions of the Torah at that time.

18. Francis Watson, *Paul and the Hermeneutics of Faith* (London: T&T Clark, 2004), 251.

19. Sandmel, *Philo of Alexandria*, 59.

20. Erwin R. Goodenough, *Introduction to Philo Judaeus*, 2nd ed. (New York: Barnes & Noble, 1963), 52–74.

21. Philo seems to suggest that the law of nature remains superior to the written law, in that the earthly copy can never match the heavenly one.

22. Philo, *Abr.* 1.4–5.

23. Samuel Sandmel, *Philo's Place in Judaism: A Study of the Conceptions of Abraham in Jewish Literature* (Cincinnati: Hebrew Union College Press, 1956), 107.

24. Ibid., 178–79.

25. Robert Jewett, *Romans: A Commentary* (Minneapolis: Fortress Press, 2007), 331.

26. James H. Charlesworth, ed., *The Old Testament Pseudepigrapha* (New York: Doubleday, 1983), 2:555.

27. The model is taken from a tradition that interprets Isaac's silence at the altar (Gen. 22:9-10) as an indication that he accepted his sacrifice without complaint. In *Liber antiquitatum biblicarum* (Pseudo-Philo) 32.3, the same view is expressed in a speech attributed to Isaac: "What and if I had not been born in the world to be offered a sacrifice unto him that made me?"

28. In *Jewish Antiquities*, Josephus claims that he neither adds to nor deletes anything from Scripture (*Ant.* 1.17; 4.197; 8.56; 10.218), yet he does both. See Harold W. Attridge, *The Interpretation of Biblical History in the Antiquitates Judaicae of Flavius Josephus* (Missoula, MT: Scholars Press, 1976), 57–60.

29. For an elaboration of this, see Sandmel, *Philo's Place*, 76. However, Sandmel does not find this propaganda motif for Abraham.

30. Sandmel, *Philo's Place*, 75, asserts that Josephus suggests that Abraham is a kind of Greek philosopher, but he never develops this concept. Louis H. Feldman argues that Josephus attributes to Abraham what Greek philosophers claimed to be the ideal qualities of a philosopher, in *Transactions and Proceedings of the American Philosophical Association* 99 (1968): 143–56.

31. Louis H. Feldman, "Hellenizations in Josephus' Jewish Antiquities: The Portrait of Abraham," in *Josephus, Judaism and Christianity*, ed. Louis H. Feldman and Gohei Hata (Detroit: Wayne State University Press, 1987), 137.

32. In *Ant.* 1.154–55, Josephus states that Abraham "was therefore the first who dared to declare that God was the sole Creator of everything and that, if other things contributed something to humankind's happiness, each one supplies something in accordance with His command and not by its own strength."

33. Josephus, *Ant.* 1.155–56.

34. Louis H. Feldman, *Abraham the Greek Philosopher in Josephus* (New York: American Philological Association, 1968), 144–45, 151–52.

35. It is noteworthy that the journeys of Aeneas in books 1.8–11 are developed in an analogous fashion with the wanderings of Abraham in Genesis 1–22. See *Aeneid* 1.33; 1.8–11

36. Steve Mason, ed., *Judean Antiquities: Translation and Commentary* (Leiden: Brill, 2000), 3:61.517

37. Josephus, *Ant.* 1.165–68. See Louis H. Feldman, *Josephus's Interpretation of the Bible* (Berkeley: University of California Press, 1968), chap. 6, "Abraham," where Josephus describes Abraham's interactions in Egypt as the head of one school of Hellenistic philosophy disputing with the head of a rival school, 230.

38. For a clear understanding of the role and place of Aeneas, see the introduction of this book.

39. Attridge, *Interpretation*, 71–72.

40. F. H. Sanbach, *The Stoics* (New York: Norton, 1975), 69.

6

Conclusion and Implications

The argument of this work has been to describe how Paul's construction of Abraham in Romans assisted Africans to appreciate Christianity, not as a foreign religion, but as one that was in alignment with African traditional religion. The Aeneas-Abraham paradigm is new, and it fits the experience of African Christianity. This comparison is powerful because Paul did what Christians do. He did not just walk onto the scene seeking to impose his Jewish ancestry. Rather, he selectively appropriated aspects of the *Aeneid* story and made them central to his Jesus story. Therefore, the creative action out of a situation of encounter and collision between cultures is a point of solid comparison and analogy between Paul and the African experience. The implication of this comparison leads to two fundamental theological views. First, I would propose to my fellow postcolonial African Christians that Paul did exactly what we have done. In the Old Testament, we see that God is referred to as "God of the patriarchs," and after reading the vernacular Bible, Africans saw similar references in which God is referred to as "God of the ancestors."

Second, I would say to Euro-American New Testament scholars that because I come out of the experience of Shona Christianity, I understand something about Paul that they have not yet seen. The genealogical tree found in Matt. 1:1–17 and the one Paul revisits in Romans 4 must be taken into account when doing a theological exegesis of Paul. I believe that when New Testament scholars take into account the genealogies found in the Bible, there will be a transformation in the way cultures will begin to appropriate the message of the Bible. The revelation of God has always been through ancestral figures, and to ignore that aspect makes it difficult to formulate a reasonable theological account of God's revelation in Jesus Christ. In this case, culture continues to be a formidable force in biblical interpretation. On the one hand, Roman poets and writers such as Dionysius of Halicarnassus and Virgil strove to maintain the ideological stance that emperors and the ruling elites were guardians and champions of Rome's *mos maiorum*. On the other hand, Diaspora Jewish historians—namely, Philo and Josephus—saw it as their responsibility to preserve, maintain, and guard the metanarrative*s* of their ancestors. In these two Jewish historians, Abraham was an ancient figure who abandoned astrology in Chaldea, migrated to Palestine under divine inspiration, sought wisdom, and ultimately achieved perfection in his piety toward God. Like any other ancient Greco-Roman ancestor, Abraham lived and practiced all the cardinal virtues. Thus Abraham embodied all the elements of Hellenistic heroes. What this book has proven is that ancestors, or *nostri maiores*, are central to identity formation. In Rom. 4:1-25, Paul creatively constructs Abraham as an ancestor of all peoples, nations, and races. We as African Christians already felt an affinity for Paul's notion of ancestry, and we creatively selected aspects of Western Christianity and appropriated them into our African colonial and postcolonial Christianity. In the same way, Paul's appeal to Abraham is a counter to the *Aenied.* There is no doubt that the *Aeneid* was the dominant ancestry—the "imperial ancestry"— of Paul's day, and he opposed it with Abraham. The *Aeneid*, as I have argued, was meant to establish the propaganda of Augustus anchored in the Trojan legend.

Theologically and sociologically, Africans recognize that humanity does not live in isolation, but there is always a community of both the living and the dead.[1] The community is guided by ancestors, who are invoked at all times, and the loss of ancestral connections is one of the most devastating experiences of many Africans. Thus humanity is part of this entire process of evolution, and all individuals belong to a family of the living and the dead. New Testament commentaries and exegeses, especially on Paul's Epistle to the Romans, must take into account the centrality of kinship, which the Roman elite of the Augustan era sought to guard, protect, and establish as the foundation of the empire. The appropriation of Abraham's ancestry into African Christianity is thus a major new development in New Testament theology.

The New Testament, whether read from an African or Western perspective, furnishes the best tractate on the testament of ancestors of faith who in their daily living modeled how humanity should conduct its life in this world and in the world to come.[2] Read in African vernacular terms, the Bible shows the ancestors as a coordinate, measuring time in generations, which again is an African concept. What now remains is to offer some similarities and differences between Aeneas and Abraham and to show the theological implications of this comparison in the postcolonial exegesis of Paul among Africans.

Aeneas and Abraham: A Comparison

The similarity between Aeneas and Abraham cannot be doubted, especially when one takes into account what I have referred to as the canonical texts of the book of Genesis and the *Aeneid*. Aeneas and Abraham are patriarchs, founders, and ancestors of their peoples: the Israelites on one hand and Romans on the other. The two were chosen by the divine for their missions, and promises were given to both for eternity. These founding ancestors had salvific significance not only to their own people but for all who would come under their imperial influence. Both Hellenistic and Jewish traditions claimed great allegiance to ancestors, a model that resonates perfectly well with other ancestral cultures of the world, especially the Shona ethnic groups of Zimbabwe. The creative exegesis of Genesis 12–22 and Paul's Epistle to the Romans makes it clear that Paul reconstructed Abraham to be the "ancestor" of believing nations and thus countered the imperial ideology of Greeks and Romans, who had created a hero out of a family man, forging him as a link between a divine power and a chosen people.

The call and journeys of Abraham are clearly documented in Genesis 12–22, and the same narrative appears in the *Aeneid*, books 1–9, especially in book 5, where the title of Aeneas is elevated from "pious Aeneas" to "Father Aeneas." Both narratives take the figures from their cradle, and they wander under a divine promise. Abraham, like Aeneas, leaves his home and his ancestral country and listens to the voice of the divine, which calls him to an undetermined place. In both figures, the narratives play an important role as they portray a life of faith which defines the journey. The departures of Abraham and Aeneas should be seen not only as historical narratives but also as theological narratives that embrace all nations, races, and peoples of the world. The story of the two ancestors points each to three areas of life: past, present, and future. In each case, the future is always hinted at, and the existence of descendants before God was to be informed by such a background. The life of *pietas*/*fides*/faith keeps both ancestors in pursuit of the new lands, thus enabling other diverse cultures of the world to creatively appropriate their stories. In similar fashion, both figures are patriarchs and founding fathers of their nations, namely, the Jews and the Romans. Yet neither of them was born as a member of his respective people. For both sides are appropriated and constructed by foreign cultures.

Therefore, a connection of both of these ancestors to their peoples is, in certain respects, tenuous or uncertain. Abraham was not born an Israelite any more than Aeneas was born a Roman. Abraham was originally a rich Chaldean, while Aeneas was a poor Trojan whose land was attacked by foreign invaders.

In relation to their peoples, both figures were foreigners and not of the same religious traditions. Abraham, like Aeneas, represents the motif of the wanderer, but also the phenomenon of the foreigner or alien. Indeed, these elements are constitutive of their respective identities, not only in an anthropological sense but also in a societal and theological sense.

Abraham and Aeneas are ideological constructs that contribute to the formation of nations. But their nations differed in that Abraham's was always in exile, and Aeneas's founded and established the Roman Empire.[3] They share this function of nation formation not only with Heracles and Odysseus but also with other Mediterranean and Asian heroes, of whom there are many legends, not the least of which was the Gilgamesh epic. Abraham and Aeneas were not given the power to rule other people but to exercise wisdom with the cultures they encountered. In Aeneas's case, the power was to be exercised wisely, with restraint and compassion, thereby enabling Rome's subject peoples to contribute to, as well as share in, the adornments of a powerful civilization.

The Aeneas and Abraham legends present an idealistic vision of world reconciliation befitting the call. Both Aeneas and Abraham are ideological, social, political, and religious constructs. Ideologically, the powerful can manipulate this for their benefit, thus turning ancestors into icons of "gold and glory."[4] Being "chosen" could slip into manipulativeness, self-assurance into arrogance, and high station into lust for wealth and material benefit. This was the case especially with Aeneas, whom Virgil used to authenticate Augustan propaganda.

Abraham and Aeneas were both called to their missions by the divine.[5] Their missions involved embracing other nations, thereby promoting an interdependence of nations, continents, genders, races, cultures, and political and economic systems. Aeneas not only shows the elements of a wanderer but also shares the Abrahamic qualities of being threatened by catastrophe and danger. In both figures, the divine intervenes to rescue and save them from danger. The intriguing element in Aeneas and Abraham is the theme of triumph over death, an element that helps them focus on their mission. In their function as ancestors, both are promised personal protection for themselves, their immediate families, and their direct descendants; they are also promised something great for their later descendants.[6] Those who claimed Abraham failed to recognize the significant fact that the founding fathers stretched out to include diverse cultures of the world. The salvation promised to Abraham was indeed for all peoples, nations, and races, who would imitate the faith of a spiritual ancestor. In Abraham, there is an emphasis on humility and openness to all cultures. In Aeneas, there is both arrogance and dominance of less privileged cultures, thus giving Rome a license to exercise imperial rule over others. In fact, what Paul does in Abraham can only be labeled as a reversal of imperial Roman values and thus makes Abraham a unique ancestor both inside and outside of the Hellenistic and Jewish world.

The Theological and Spiritual Uniqueness of Abraham

Abraham is unique in that he was not aware of his destination after he was divinely called from Chaldea. He also did not save the gods of his father but trusted in the divine command— a characteristic that Paul would creatively use in constructing the spiritual ancestry of all believing cultures. Abraham is tested in Gen. 17:17, and he is found faithful, in the sense that his obedience to the divine command completes his lifelong rejection of the idolatry of his native place.[7] Abraham's story is suffused with faith in the divinity, thus rendering him an ancestor who can fit into all believing societies of the world. The Genesis narrative attests to the validity of this claim, and theologically makes Abraham a hero of faith.

In postcolonial cultures, people invoke their ancestors and couch them within biblical narratives. Throughout Africa, Christians have adopted Abraham through music and have come to identify with him in many aspects of life. Using Paul as a theological dialogue partner, peoples can claim a new Abraham, who was at home among the rich, philosophers, the poor, and foreigners. The Shona people of Zimbabwe can easily revisit their ancient ancestral traditions and claim Abraham as their faith ancestor. They can do this by re-creating their past, retelling their stories in different shapes and amplifying the scriptural corpus itself through the medium of vernacular hermeneutics, songs, and literary forms. Music and storytelling are part of African life. Africans sing readily when they are harvesting or sawing; and even when their culture is under attack, music fulfills a social, religious, and social function. The uniqueness of Abraham's role and function in Paul's thought appears in many ways.

First, the uniqueness of Abraham among Africans is in the way God is referred to as "the God of our ancestors, Abraham, Sarah, Isaac, and Jacob." The central issue in Romans is not how Abraham was justified, but rather the revelation of the nature of God. God's relationship with Abraham can be described as "complementary," on the basis that Abraham first received the call and accepted it, and God confirmed that he would be a blessing to all nations (Gen. 12:1-8). That which began with Abraham and found its culmination in Jesus Christ continues in the modern-day church and will forever be a reality.

Abraham and, consequently, Jesus Christ founded lineages and thus carry God's grace and promises to all nations, races, and peoples.[8]

Second, Abraham's God is not an imperial figure but is transcendent as well as immanent. In their complementary relationship, God and Abraham promise to honor each other in ways that put the entire universe first. God calls Abraham to a universal responsibility—all families of the earth are the focus of God's interest. God has all nations in view, and God's purposes encompass every creature on earth. The God of Abraham seeks a relationship based on trust, and God's words have power to change lives and worlds forever. At every development, God speaks with Abraham about the future of humanity and especially about the future of Sodom and Gomorrah (Gen. 18:16-32). The God of Abraham seriously respects human participation, honoring Abraham's judgments. In other words, the God of Abraham is not far away but is close to people and approachable by all. This God is the one whom Africans had known, and yet missionaries at times preached an imperial God.

A postcolonial notion apparent in the Old Testament is that God interacts with outsiders—the powerless, such as Hagar (Gen. 16:7-14) and Abimelech (Gen. 20:3-6). This is also true of Abraham; after being called by God, he encounters foreigners—Canaanites, Egyptians, Hittites, Aramaeans, other empires such as Sodom and Gomorrah, and pre-Israelite rulers of Jerusalem (Gen. 16:7-14; 18:1—19:38; 19:37-38; 20:10-20; 21:9; 21:22-34; 25:1-18). These encompassing experiences are a confirmation of Abraham's blessing that he will be a "father of many nations" and a blessing to many. All the foreigners react positively to Abraham. Of special interest to me is Melchizedek, who blesses Abraham on God's behalf (Genesis 14). Not only that, but Abimelech exemplifies a fear of God in a manner that calls Abraham to account for his deeds; he also serves as Abraham's confessor (Genesis 20).

Implications and Relevance for New Testament Interpretations

Having rehearsed the history of African Christianity and its adaptation in the colonial and postcolonial period, it is reasonable to conclude this book by focusing on the implications and relevance of this history in the exegesis and interpretation of Paul's Epistle to the Romans. While Paul's major themes in Romans seem to contradict the Augustan propaganda, it is important not to lose sight of the formative impact of Greco-Roman culture on the gospel of Jesus Christ. As an African, I argue that Paul's theology should be understood in the cultural context, values, and ethics of a people. Africans, for example, in their affinity to ancestors, were quick to comprehend Paul's construction of Abraham as a spiritual ancestor. Thus the emergence of a new, different,

Africanized Christianity in the postcolonial period was born from an encounter of two cultures: namely, Western Christianity and African traditional religion.

As Christians seek a language in which to communicate the gospel within specific contexts, fresh images are needed to relate the gospel to life as people experience it. On the one hand, Paul accomplishes this in Romans 4, where he elevates Abraham as the ancestor of all people of faith.[9] The *Aeneid*, on the other hand, focuses on the ruling elite and the privileged few of the Roman Empire. Thus Paul managed to communicate the gospel to a people who were marginalized not only by the empire but also by exile. Rome, the place to which the last epistle of Paul was addressed, was not only the capital of the Roman Empire and thereby also the capital of the Mediterranean world and its neighboring areas, but also, at the time of Paul the center of the Caesar religion, which was firmly established.[10] People in most cultural settings have ways to adapt and appropriate the old into the new. In the African perspective, ancestors can be appropriated in ways that will bring together ethnic tribes and nations.

In order to fulfill our calling as biblical interpreters, we must appropriate the gospel in the ways we see modeled in Romans and the stories of the New Testament. The Roman Empire and the birth of the New Testament are quite inseparable in our efforts to authentically interpret the gospel in the twenty-first century. The Aeneas-Abraham paradigm and the African readings of Paul have proven to be a lens through which we can do meaningful Pauline hermeneutics among ancestral-oriented nations. Artifacts, coins, images, songs, inscriptions, tombstone epitaphs and poems, and histories from the ancient Greco-Roman and the Mediterranean world are relevant in Pauline commentaries and exegesis. We must be sensitive to the intertextuality of all peoples, nations, and races, and intentional effort must be made to value other cultures. Biblical interpretation that reduces the gospel to marketing a religious product or that imposes a foreign ideology on a less powerful culture has little to do with the gospel of the crucified and risen Jesus, or with the God of Abraham.

Notes

1. For a discussion of ancestors in Africa, see John S. Mbiti, *African Religion and Philosophy* (New York: Doubleday, 1970), 25–26.

2. See Matt. 1:1-17; Luke 1:55-56; Heb. 11:1-40.

3. See Neil Elliott, "Paul and the Politics of the Empire: Problems and Prospects," in *Paul and Politics: Ekklessia, Israel, Imperium, Interpretation*, ed. Richard A. Horsley (Harrisburg, PA: Trinity Press International, 2000), 17–39.

4. See Musa Dube, "The Postcolonial Condition of the Bible," in *Postcolonial Feminist Interpretation of the Bible* (St. Louis: Chalice, 2000), 10–11.

5. Genesis 12 and 15; *Aeneid* 1.261–96, 278–79. *His ego nec metas rerum nec tempora pono; imperium sine fine dedi* ("The empire that Rome is destined to rule is to be without limits, either temporal or spatial"), *Aeneid* 6.792–96; *Aeneid* 7 synthesizes the fulfillment of the divine promise, and *Aeneid* 8 depicts the triumphant rise of Rome in its hope of Augustan peace and reconciliation.

6. The theme of divine mission took the form of a journey that would result in the formation of a new ethnos. In the narratives of Abraham, this theme is the central narrative thread around which the entire myth is organized, culminating in Paul's interpretation of Abraham in Rom. 4:1-25.

7. Francis Watson, *Paul and the Hermeneutics of Faith* (London: T&T Clark, 2004), 225–26.

8. See Stanly Stowers, *A Rereading of Romans: Justice, Jews and Gentiles* (New Haven: Yale University Press, 1994), 230–31.

9. See chapters 2 and 3 of this book, where the concept is defined and elaborated.

10. Dieter Georgi, unpublished notes on Paul under the aspect of the Latin (2003).

Bibliography

Agamben, Giorgio. *The Time That Remains: A Commentary on the Letter to the Romans*. Stanford: Stanford University Press, 2005.

Annal di storia dell' esegesis: Come e nato il Cristianesimo? 21, no. 2 (Centro Italiano di Studi Superiori delle Religioni, 2004): 497–615.

Attridge, Harold W. *The Interpretation of Biblical History in the Antiquitates Judaicae of Flavius Josephus*. Missoula, MT: Scholars, 1976.

Banana Canaan. "The Case for a New Bible." In *Voices from the Margin: Interpreting the Bible in Third World*. ed. R. S. Surgirtharajah. New York: Orbis, 2000.

———. *The Church and the Struggle for Zimbabwe: From the Programme to Combat Racism to Combat Theology*. Gweru, Zimbabwe: Mambo Press, 1996.

———. *Rewriting the Bible: The Real Issues*. Gweru: Mambo Press, 1993.

[Bauer's] *Greek –English Lexicon of the New Testament and Other Early Christian Literature*, 3rd ed., ed. William Arndt, Frederick W. Danker, and F. Gingrich. Chicago: University of Chicago Press, 2000.

Berchman, Robert M. *From Philo to Middle Platonism in Transition*. Chico, CA: Scholars Press, 1984.

Bonz, Marianne Palmer. *The Past as Legacy: Luke-Acts and Ancient Epic*. Minneapolis: Fortress Press, 2000.

Bourdillon, M. F. C. S.J., ed. *Christianity South of the Zambezi*. Gweru: Mambo Press, 1977.

———. *The Shona Peoples: An Ethnography of the Contemporary Shona, with Special Reference to Their Religion*. Harare: Mambo Press, 1987.

Boyarin, Daniel. *A Radical Jew: Paul and the Politics of Identity*. Berkeley: University of California Press, 1994.

Bremmer, J., and N. M. Horshfall. *Roman Myth and Mythography*. London: University of London, 1987.

Brunt, P. A., and J. M. Moore, eds. *Res Gestae Divi Augusti: The Achievements of the Divine Augustu*. Oxford: Oxford University Press, 1967.

Bultmann, Rudolph. *Theology of the New Testament*. New York: Scribner, 1951.

Burnett, Andrew, Michel Amandry, and Pere Pau Ripolles, eds. *Roman Provincial Coinage: From the Death of Caesar to the Death of Vitellius (44 BC – AD 69)*. Vol. 1. London: British Museum Press, 1992.

Campbell, William S. *Paul's Gospel in an Intercultural Context: Jew and Gentile in the Letter to the Romans*. New York: Peter Lang, 1992.

Charlesworth, James H., ed. *The Old Testament Pseudepigrapha*, 2 vols. New York: Doubleday, 1983: 2:555.

Daneel, M. L. *Quest for Belonging: Introduction to a Study of African Independent Churches*. Gweru: Mambo Press, 1987.

Dillon, John M. *The Middle Platonists 80 B.C. to A.D. 220*. Ithaca, NY: Cornell University Press, 1977.

Dionysius of Halicarnassus. *Roman Antiquities Book 1*. LCL Classical Library. Cambridge University Press, 2001.

Dodge, Ralph E. *American Methodist Conference in Zambia* 3 (1938) housed at Old Mutare Mission in Zimbabwe.

———. "The African Church Now and in the Future," unpublished essay, 1966. On file at the Old Mutare Mission Church Library, Zimbabwe.

Dube, Musa. *Postcolonial Feminist Interpretation of the Bible*. St. Louis: Chalice, 2000.

Elliot, Neil. *The Arrogance of Nations: Reading Romans in the Shadow of the Empire.* Minneapolis: Fortress Press, 2008.

Esler, Philip. *New Testament Theology: Communion and Community.* Minneapolis: Fortress, 2005.

Feldman, Louis H. *Abraham the Greek Philosopher in Josephus.* New York: American Philological Association, 1968.

———. "Hellenizations in Josephus' Jewish Antiquities: The Portrait of Abraham." In *Josephus, Judaism and Christianity,* ed. Feldman and Gohei Hata. Detroit: Wayne State University Press, 1987.

———. *Josephus's Interpretation of the Bible.* Berkeley: University of California Press, 1968.

———. *Judaism and Hellenism Reconsidered.* Leiden: Brill: 2006.

———. *Transactions and Proceedings of the American Philosophical Association* 99 (1968): 143–56.

Field, D. M. *Greek and Roman Mythology.* New York: Chartwell, 1977.

Friedrich, Gerhard. *Theological Dictionary of the New Testament*, vol. 6. Grand Rapids, MI: Wm. B. Eerdmans., 1968.

Galinsky, G. Karl. *Aeneas, Sicily, and Rome.* Princeton, NJ: Princeton University Press, 1969.

Garnsey, Peter, and Richard Saller, eds. *The Roman Empire: Economy, Society and Culture.* Berkeley: University of California, 1987.

Georgi, Dieter. *Die Gegner des Paulus im 2. Korntherbrief.* Assen: Neukirchener, 1964.

———. "Paul," unpublished manuscript (2003).

———. *Theocracy in Paul's Praxis*, trans. Davil L. Green. Minneapolis: Fortress, 1991.

———. "Who is the True Prophet?" *Harvard Theological Review* 79 (1986): 1–3.

Goodenough, Erwin R. *Introduction to Philo Judaeus,* 2nd ed. New York: Barnes & Noble, 1963.

Gruen, Erik S. *Culture and National Identity in Republican Rome.* New York: Cornell University Press, 1992.

———. "The Making of the Trojan Legend." In *Culture and National Identity in Republican Rome*. Ithaca: Cornell University Press, 1992.

———. *Heritage and Hellenism: The Reinvention of Jewish Tradition.* Berkeley: University of California Press, 1998.

Harrison, J. R. "Paul, Eschatology and the Augustan Age of Grace," *TynBul* 50 (1999): 79-91.

Hays, Richard B. *Echoes of Scripture in the Letters of Paul.* New Haven: Yale University Press, 1989.

Hengel, Martin. *Judaism and Hellenism: Studies in the Encounter during the Early Hellenistic Period.* Eugene, OR: Wipf & Stock, 2003.

Homer. *Iliad.* LCL Classical Library, Book 20. Cambridge: Harvard University Press, 1968.

"Paul and the Politics of the Empire: Problems and Prospects." In *Paul and Politics: Ekklessia, Israel, Imperium, Interpretatio*, ed. Richard A. Horsley. Harrisburg, PA: Trinity Press International, 2000.

The Internet Classic Archive, "The Aeneid by Virgil," trans. John Dryden, at http://classics.mit.edu/Virgil/aeneid.1.i.html

Jewett, Robert. *Romans: Hermeneia—A Critical and Historical Commentary on the Bible*. Minneapolis: Fortress, 2007.

Josephus, Flavius. *Jewish Antiquities*. Books 1-3. Cambridge: Harvard University Press, 1998.

Jowitt, Harold. "The Annual Report of the Director of Native Education" (1928), 15, found at the University of Zimbabwe Library.

Justin. *Dialogus cum Tryphone.* New York: Walter de Gruyter, 1979.

Kahl, Brigitte. *Galatians Re-Imagined: Reading with the Eyes of the Vanquished.* Minneapolis: Fortress, 2010.

Kamudzandu, Israel. *Abraham as Spiritual Ancestor: A Postcolonial Zimbabwe Reading of Romans 4.* Leiden: Brill, 2010.

Kapenzi, Geoffrey Z. *The Clash of Cultures: Christian Missionaries and the Shona of Rhodesia.* Washington, DC: University Press of America, 1978.

Kasemann, Ernst. *Perspectives on Paul.* Philadelphia: Fortress, 1971.

Kurewa, John Wesley Z. *The Church in Mission: A Short History of the United Methodist Church in Zimbabwe, 1897–1997.* Nashville: Abingdon, 1997.

———. *Preaching and Cultural Identity: Proclaiming the Gospel in Africa.* Nashville: Abingdon, 2000.

Lang, Andrew. *Making Religion.* New York: Longman, Green, 1889.

Livingstone, David. *Missionary Travels and Researches in South Africa.* London, 1857.

Livy. *Condition of the Urban Situation.* In aedibus. B.G: Teubneri, 1981. Cambridge: Harvard University Press, 1988.

Lopez, Davina C. *Apostle to the Conquered: Reimagining Paul's Mission.* Minneapolis: Fortress Press, 2008.

MacMullen, Ramsay. *Romanization in The Time of Augustus.* New Haven: Yale University Press, 2000.

Martin, Dale B. *The Corinthian Body.* New Haven and London: Yale University Press, 1995.

Martin, David, and Phyllis Johnson. *The Struggle for Zimbabwe: The Chimurenga War*. New York: Monthly Review Press, 1981.

Mason, Steve, ed. *Judean Antiquities: Translation and Commentary*. Leiden: Brill, 2000.

Mbiti, John S. *African Religion and Philosophy*. New York: Doubleday, 1970.

Missionary Review of the World 17, no. 12 (1894): 882.

Momigliano, Arnold. *On Pagans, Jews, and Christians*. Middletown, CT: Wesleyan University Press, 1987.

Monk, Edwin ed. *Dr. Livingstone's Cambridge Lectures* (1858; report., Farnborough, Eng.: Gregg International, 1968), 170 (February 15, 1859).

Mungazi, Dickson A. *Colonial Education for Africans: George Stark's Policy in Zimbabwe*. New York: Praeger, 1991.

———. *The Honored Crusade: Ralph Dodge's Theology of Liberation and Initiative for Social Change in Zimbabwe*. Gweru: Mambo Press, 1991.

Murphree, Marshall W. *Christianity and the Shona*. Gweru: Mambo Press, 1969.

Mwamuka, Aldon. Presidential address during an annual conference of the African Teachers Association, Mutare (July 31, 1945), in the Zimbabwean National Archives.

Needham, D. E., E. K. Mashingaidze, and N. Bhebhe, eds. *From Iron Age to Independence: A History of Central Africa*. Harare: Longman, 1984.

Ngoma dze United Methodist Church Ye Zimbabwe, or Hymns of the United Methodist Church in Zimbabwe. Harare: United Methodist Press, 1964.

Ngugi Wa Thiong'o. *Decolonizing the Mind: The Politics of Language in African Literature*. Nairobi, Kenya: East African Educational Publishers, 1986.

Niebuhr, H. Richard. *Christ and Culture*. New York: Harper, 1956.

O' Farrell, T. A. "Report to Annual Conference," *Official Journal of the Methodist Church* (1928): 30, found in the United Methodist Archive at Old Mutare Mission in Zimbabwe.

Ranger, Terence. *Voices from the Rocks: Nature, Culture and History in the Matopos Hills of Zimbabwe.* Bloomington: Indiana University Press, 1999.

Said, Edward. *Orientalism.* New York: Vintage, 1978.

Sanbach, F. H. *The Stoics.* New York: Norton, 1975.

Sandmel, Samuel. *Philo of Alexandria: An Introduction.* Oxford: Oxford University Press, 1979.

———. *Philo's Place in Judaism: A Study of the Conceptions of Abraham in Jewish Literature.* Cincinnati: Hebrew Union College Press, 1956.

Simpson, D. P. *Casell's Compact Latin Dictionary.* New York: Dell, 1963.

Stegemann, Wolfgang. "The Emergence of God's New People: The Beginnings of Christianity Reconsidered," *HTS Theological Studies/ Teologiese Studies* 62, no. 1 (2006). [a]http://www.journals.co.za/ej/ejour_hervorm.html)

Stone, Michael E., trans. *The Testament of Abraham: The Greek Recensions.* Missoula, MT: Society of Biblical Literature, 1972.

Stowers, Stanley Kent. *A Rereading of Romans: Justice, Jews and Gentiles.* New Haven: Yale University Press, 1994.

Tanner, Marie. *The Last Descendant of Aeneas: The Hapsburgs and the Mythic Image of the Emperor.* New Haven: Yale University Press, 1993.

Van Ruitten, J. T. A. G. M. "Abraham, Job and the Book of Jubilees." In *The Sacrifice of Isaac: The Aqedah (Genesis 22) and Its Interpretations,* ed. Eibert Tigchelar and Ed Noort. Leiden: Brill, 2002.

Virgil. *The Aeneid.* English translation from *The Internet Classic Archive,* "The Aeneid by Virgil," trans. John Dryden. http://classics.mit.edu/Virgil/aeneid.1.i.html

von Rad, Gerhard. *Genesis: A Commentary.* London: SCM, 1972.

Wagenvoort, H. "Pietas." In *Studies in Greek and Roman Religion*, vol. 1, ed. H. S. Versnell. Leiden: Brill, 1980.

Wallace, David R. *The Gospel of God: Rome as Paul's Aeneid.* Eugene, Oregon: Pickwick Publications, 2008.

Wallace-Hadrill, Andrew. "Knowing the Ancestors." In *Rome's Cultural Revolution,* ed. Andrew Wallace-Hadrill. Cambridge: Cambridge University Press, 2008.

———. *Rome's Cultural Revolution.* Cambridge: Cambridge University Press, 2008.

Watson, Francis. *Paul and the Hermeneutics of Faith.* London: T&T Clark International, 2004.

Western, D. The *Value of the African Past: The International Review of Missions.* London: Oxford University Press, 1926.

Wheeler, Brannon M. *Prophets in the Quran: An Introduction to the Quran and Muslim Exegesis.* London: Continuum, 2002.

White, John L. *The Apostle of God: Paul and the Promise of Abraham.* Massachusetts: Hendrickson Publishers, 1999.

Wisemann, T. P. *The Myths of Rome.* Devon, UK: University of Exeter Press, 2004.

Witherington, Ben, III. *Conflict and Community in Corinth: A Socio-Rhetorical Commentary on 1 and 2 Corinthians.* Grand Rapids, MI: Wm. B. Eerdmans, 1995.

Wright, N. T. *The Resurrection of the Son of God.* Minneapolis: Fortress Press, 2003.

Zanker, Paul. *The Power of Images in the Age of Augustus.* Ann Arbor: University of Michigan Press, 1990.

Index of Names

Index of Passages